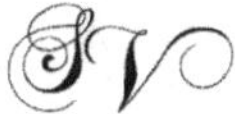

NIGHTINGALE

SAY GOODBYE TO YESTERDAY

TONY LOPES

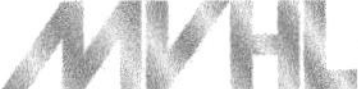

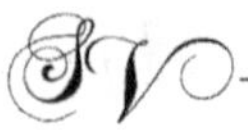

NIGHTINGALE: Say Goodbye to Yesterday

Creative contribution by Jennifer Plaza and Carol McManus.
Cover Design - Low & Joe Creative, Brea, CA 92821
Book Layout - DBree, StoneBear Design

Manufactured and printed in the United States of America distributed globally by markvictorhansenlibrary.com

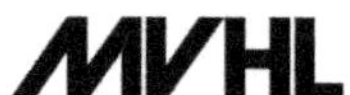

New York | Los Angeles | London | Sydney

ISBN: 979-8-88581-056-2 Hardback
ISBN: 979-8-88581-057-9 Paperback
ISBN: 979-8-88581-058-6 eBook
Library of Congress Control Number: 2022916286

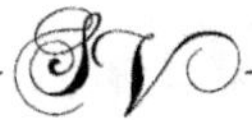

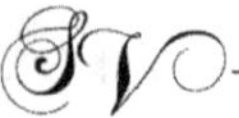

The Savannah Valley Series

Everyone imagines what life will be like in retirement. Perhaps you know someone who ended up in a depressing nursing facility with people who didn't care about their health and wellbeing. That's not the way it has to be and that's not the way it is in Savannah Valley.

The characters in these books celebrate life and retirement in fun and imaginative ways after facing unexpected challenges. Here, new friendships are made, new horizons open, and a lifetime of experience and acquired wealth is celebrated.

Each book in the series is inspired by true events unique to each author. Sit back, relax, and allow yourself to be transported to the glorious and prestigious retirement community known as Savannah Valley.

Nightingale : Say Goodbye to Yesterday
by Tony Lopes

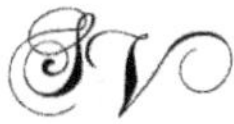

All About Henry : Rich Widower of Savannah Valley
by Lyle Lee Jenkins

Love After : Dreams Still Come True
by Russell Gray & Mona Guarino

Maestro : Songteller of Savannah Valley
by Rick & Stacie Fessler

Rich Widows of Savannah Valley
by Mitzi Perdue

Ruby : Magic Comes From the Heart
by Randall Kenneth Jones

markvictorhansenlibrary.com/savannah-valley

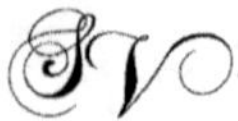

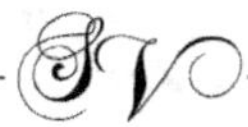

CONTENTS

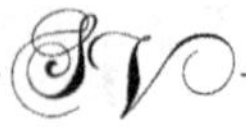

DEDICATION

No one has a crystal ball. And life can change on a dime. This book is dedicated to those that have pushed through the challenges and to those that have yet to face those challenges. We understand your struggles, we stand with you. *Nightingale* serves as an inspirational message, providing guidance and hope for a meaningful and bright future that you deserve.

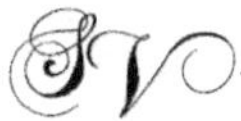

PROLOGUE

Would you want to know how much time you have left on this planet? Some do, some don't. Regardless of your stance, the philosophical question of how to live your best life, how to make a positive impact on those around you and the legacy you leave to the next generation, weighs ever more on us as we age.

In this story, you will see how Adelia, my mother, struggles with these questions. The same questions you and those around you are facing. *Nightingale* is not about me. Nor is it really about Adelia. It's about you. It's about you living your best life. And having a great positive impact on those around you. And most certainly looking back on what could've been done differently in life and sharing that learning with the next generation.

Our journey in life is one of uncertainty to a great extent. Sure, we can plan for certain life-events but you, I and Adelia still had hurdles to overcome regardless of all our great planning. Why do some navigate these hurdles better than others? Perhaps *Nightingale* will provide some answers, as I suspect you will resonate with the many twists and turns of Adelia's story.

Adelia's story is an inspirational message that I know you will love. *Nightingale* has the potential to change lives from despair to one of adventure, hope and opportunity.

After all, don't we all just want to live out our best life?

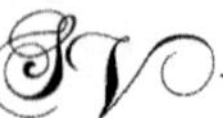

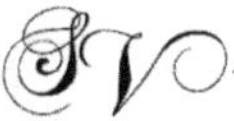

CHAPTER 1
AZALEAS

"Why are you doing this? You love teaching. What will Dartmouth do without you?" Charlotte cried. She dabbed at the tears threatening to ruin her mascara. "Christopher, you know Mom doesn't want to leave."

Adelia went to her youngest daughter and wrapped her arms around the frantic young woman. "I've lost the house, Charlotte, dear. Your father's medical expenses were just too much for me to keep up. Christopher assured me that this retirement community is unlike any other." She sighed into her daughter's soft auburn hair. "Samantha, come console your sister while I finish checking the packing list."

Samantha, Adelia's middle daughter, took her mother's place, hugging her sister. "Seriously, Chris, why didn't you at least pay off the house. We wouldn't be having this conversation. You know Charlotte has enough anxiety."

"I tried; you know that. Mom didn't want a handout," Christopher said. He sat in the mauve Chippendale wingback, tucked in the bedroom corner. "They took out a mortgage on the house to pay the medical expenses. There's no equity left. That's why she turned the keys over to the bank. Tell them, ma."

Adelia sat on the edge of the bed. The side where her husband Ted breathed his last, a mere three weeks prior. She kept their financial struggles from the children, until hiding the magnitude dictated otherwise. Both she and Ted decided to let the mortgage payments go, believing his treatments would cure his colon cancer. But life had other plans. He passed from a myocardial infarction. She'd awoken to find him gone, slipped away in eternal sleep.

"Mom," The oldest of her children was tuned in on a tablet, via Facebook Live from her own home in Los Angeles, "Ma. Is she listening?"

"I am, Michelle," Adelia sighed. She folded the sheet of paper on which she wrote her moving notes.

"Mom, I agree with Sam and Charlotte. This is a major change. You and Daddy spent your whole adult life in Hanover, New Hampshire. Do you think you can live in Georgia?" she cringed. "Georgia, mom."

Christopher stood up and glared at the tablet. "What are you three doing? This is not your decision. This is what mom wants." He crossed his arms with an audible sigh, "Listen, I wouldn't let Mom go just anywhere. I bought her a house in Savannah Valley. It's a beautiful place in a warm climate. Plus, it's a great investment."

"Not okay, Chris. I don't want Mom shipped off to some community," Sam hissed.

Adelia sat between her two daughters and propped

the tablet on the nightstand. She waved for Christopher to come closer. She clasped her hands in her lap, taking a steadying breath. "Kids. I never imagined taking money from my children. Michelle, you've got an amazing career as a producer, living the Hollywood life and it's very expensive there. Sam, you live in Michigan and you're a professor like your father and I were. I know how much money you make. And Charlotte, you just signed a lease on a property in Paris and you're just starting your career. Chris is in New York working for Douglas and Douglas Investments and he pointed out he is the only one with any financial independence."

Charlotte interrupted, "So just because he has more money than us, he has to run your life?"

"That's not fair," Chris protested.

"Stop it, all of you." Adelia lowered her voice. "Chris believes that retirement should provide a quality of life and by investing in real estate, this will be an asset that will grow. The fact that Christopher bought a house for me in Georgia wrenches my stomach into knots. But he's right. This is what I want. You all have your own lives now," she reminded. "Where do I fit in?"

The three women remained silent.

Adelia peered up at Christopher. "I have nothing to keep me here. I can take retirement and I'll have a good pension. Remember, we paid on this house all these years, the house you all grew up in. It was going to be foreclosed and I think that's the sign that told me now is the time for me to move on, too. Besides, while on sabbatical I lost my passion for teaching. I'm ready for a change. And your father and I always dreamed of moving south. To get away from teaching, the cold, and snow." Chris knelt on the beige carpet before his mother. His tailored Alfani suit pulled tight at the thighs. The material was a stark contrast to the light colors of the room. Adelia put her hand on his shoulder. "Enough talk. Let's have a pleasant dinner before we leave for Savannah Valley. Chris and I leave for the airport at six tomorrow morning."

She stood, kissing each on the head and blowing an additional kiss to Michelle on video wiping a tear from her eye. Her children were strong willed and pushed their opinions to the point of no return. She knew that. It was their way—even in childhood. When she clicked the door closed behind her, their voices rose. She pressed her back against the heavy oaken door. *What is Christopher getting me into?* she thought. *I hope I'm making the right decision.*

The movers were in the living room. The baby grand piano Adelia kept from her mother's estate was wrapped and loaded into the truck. Everything was boxed, labeled, and secured. It was a job she wouldn't have been able to complete on her own. She was grateful for professional movers Chris insisted on hiring. She scanned the walls.

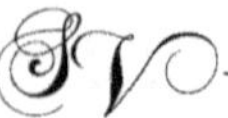

Her favorite landscape was missing. "Have you packed the *House on the Green* painting already?" she asked one of the female workers.

The woman nodded. "It is wrapped and loaded. Do you want me to show you?"

"No," Adelia declined. "Thank you. It was our piece, my husband's, and mine. The one and only piece of fine art we bought." She shook her head, laughing. "I'm sorry. You have a job to do. I'm in the way." She wandered to her bare kitchen, except for a few yet untaped boxes. She ran her hand over the pink granite counter and opened the drawer where she kept her stationary, but it was empty. Everything she knew was put in neat boxes. *A whole lifetime summed into cardboard and moving blankets crammed into a fifty-three-foot tractor trailer,* she thought.

The upstairs door slammed, footfalls thumped down the oak steps onto the foyer's tongue and groove hardwood floor. From the steps she knew it was Sam. She recognized all the patters of the kids' feet as they grew up in their humble New Hampshire oasis. The home was a two-story farmhouse, remodeled to include a foyer and open kitchen and dining area. She walked to the pantry and ran her hand over the door trim. Each of the kids' growth was recorded with a color-coded system. She liked Red for Michelle because she was Adelia's firecracker. Sam had blue for being the trusty mini mom. Charlotte was orange because she was a ball of emotions with flares like the sun. Adelia stared up at the last measurement for Christopher. He measured in at six feet three inches. She had to stand on a stool to mark his line in green. She chose green because he always seemed to make money—even when he was a small boy selling baggies of chocolate chip cookies from his wagon.

"There you are," Sam said. "We're ready to go to dinner if you are." She leaned against the counter, scanning the empty kitchen. "Are you going to be okay?"

Adelia folded her lips and nodded. "Yeah, I think I will. I trust Christopher."

• • •

Six arrive early. Adelia and Christopher were on the road to the airport in Manchester. Their flight was scheduled for ten, but they knew to arrive early. After climbing in Christopher's rental car, she checked the flight schedule, no delays. She didn't look back to see her family's home disappear behind them. It took all she had to keep her emotions in check. Her eyes were dry, but so was her mouth. She tucked her hands beneath her legs to keep from trembling.

Chris put his hand on her thigh. "You're going to be fine. We'll make it in time to grab an early dinner at their highest rated restaurant, the Sky." He patted her leg. "The reservations are already set."

“I never thought our life would turn out like this. Don’t get me wrong. I loved every moment with all of you. But to work our whole lives, building a career to have it thrown away by medical calamity. Losing our home, and then my hometown. It’s overwhelming.” She settled back in the seat and closed her eyes.

They arrived at the airport a quarter past eight. Chris stopped for coffee and danishes at Adelia’s request. It would be her last meal in New Hampshire. The flight posted a thirty-minute delay. Adelia used the time to scroll through her phone on the Savannah Valley website. Rolling green fields dotted with clusters of manicured homes filled the banner. She clicked on Sky under the dining tab and reviewed the menu. “What kind of retirement facility serves Wagyu beef?”

“Yours,” Chris smiled.

Mother and son boarded the plane and were off to the Savannah-Hilton Head International Airport. They sat in coach because Adelia wouldn’t let Chris pay for her ticket. He was adamant about buying the house, so much so, that he bought it before her agreeing. Their heated exchange swirled in her mind.

“You are not renting an apartment to live alone with no security, no anything. You won’t let me pay off the mortgage, you won’t let me settle Dad’s debt. Give me this one thing, I’m begging you. At the very least, do it for my peace

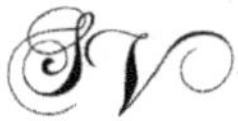

of mind." His voice betrayed the tears she imagined trickling down his cheeks.

"I can't let you do that. One day, you'll understand. Your children are not supposed to provide for you. Not when you've spent your whole life ensuring they had everything to pave their own path."

"Please, mom, I know a place. It will be a good real estate investment if nothing else. I can't lose, and neither can you. Think of this as generational wealth. One day I'll retire, and I can move to Savannah Valley."

Adelia relented. "You have your father's smarts for economics. Since you insist, and because it won't be taking from you, I guess. But no condos. Please."

She stared out the window at the landscape below. She knew it made him happy, but she was not—at least not yet. Dartmouth was her life before Ted was diagnosed. She worked years before becoming the Art History Department Chair. Retiring was not what she thought her sabbatical would lead to. No, she had plans. She figured retirement was at a minimum eleven years off. The day was bound to come. *But so sudden?* she thought.

The plane landed. The peach state's sun and lush vegetation greeted them. Upon exiting the airport, an emerald-green, metallic Mercedes S-Class sedan pulled up beside them. A woman climbed out with a tablet.

"Mrs. Adelia Franklin?"

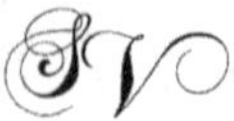

Perplexed, Adelia answered. "Yes."

"Here is your key fob. Just sign here." The woman handed Adelia the device.

Adelia signed on the line as she glanced at Christopher, an impish grin on his face. "Christopher. What did you do?" She turned to face him as the young woman walked away. "Explain."

Chris hurried around to the passenger side to open her door. "Ladies first." He left the door open and hurried back to the driver's side. "Let's just say I don't want you stranded."

Adelia slid into the passenger seat. "A Mercedes Chris? What were you thinking?" She ran her hand over the dash and the brown leather seat. "How much was this?"

"More than flying first class would have cost," he teased.

She frowned at him. "We could have just driven my Volvo."

"Your Volvo wouldn't have made it across the New Hampshire border. We're lucky we sold it to Donna for her grandson at your going away party. It's a great project car." Chris started the Mercedes and headed toward center city. "You've always wanted to see Savannah. Let's take a quick drive through before heading to Savannah Valley."

As he drove, Adelia studied the electronic dash and console. "I'm going to have to learn how to drive all over again."

"Just keep it between the lines," Chris mused. "You going to look up? You're missing everything." He drove through historic downtown Savannah, with the stately white and brick buildings. He pointed at the riverboat docked where a tour group was embarking. He turned right and navigated through historic homes lining the side streets.

She watched as they passed stately live oaks and magnolia trees. The flora was new, but familiar. She always wanted to visit Savannah. "This is gorgeous," she whispered. "It's like a botanical marriage of North and South."

"Imagine painting a cityscape here. You have a new muse." Chris maneuvered through the city and made it to the open roads on the outskirts, heading Northwest. "Ready to see your new home, mom?"

The rolling hills were carpeted in a blend of greens. As they drove over a stone arched bridge, Adelia pointed out of her window. "There's a glass building in the middle of nothing."

"That's where we are eating dinner tonight," Chris smirked.

"What?" Adelia strained to look as they circled away from the tower. In front of them the small town with iron work and cobblestones gave way to a large archway with scrolled letters welcoming them to Savannah Valley. Chris pulled up to the security gate and handed the man his phone with the pass-code. The guard waved him through. Chris eased on the accelerator and let his mother take in the fountain, expansive golf course, and glass façade on the Sky Tower. He drove past it all until they reached a fork in the road. He turned right, opposite the condo tower. Mansions of varying sizes were set back on the magnolia-lined roadway.

Adelia bit her lip. “Chris, what is this place?”

“This is Savannah Valley, and this is your new home.” He pulled up to a white multi-column antebellum mansion with an attached atrium. The sidewalk from the outbuilding to the house was lined with azaleas. A single magnolia tree stood in the front yard.

“It’s our painting! Chris, I can’t believe you found this.” Adelia exclaimed. When he parked the car in the circular drive, she hopped out to take in the whole of the house before her.

“Do you like it?” he asked.

Tears rolled down her cheeks. “I love it. I wish your father was here to see this.”

Before they had a chance to go inside, a pink golf cart buzzed by. Two women with wide brimmed white hats and pastel sundresses craned to look at Adelia and Chris. They stopped the cart, took a picture, and drove back from where they came. The house across the street was set back with a weeping willow in the front. Her new neighbor hurried

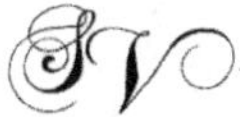

down her driveway in a white jogging suit, a pair of white platform shoes and a Yorkshire terrier tucked under her arm. She hurried to where Adelia and Chris stood.

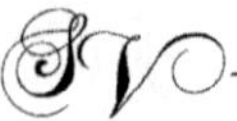

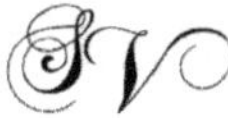

CHAPTER 2

Magnolia Street

The woman approached Adelia; her steps heavy, purposeful. The yorkie bounced against the woman's arm with each footfall. Its diamond studded blue collar reflected the afternoon sun that cast a rainbow of spots on the woman's white jogging suit. She reached her destination, positioned in front of the mother and son. She offered her hand to Adelia. "I'm Margaret Thurnwell. I live just there." She pointed at the house directly across the street. It was as large as Adelia's new home, if not a smidge larger. A pale lemon pudding of a color, triple story mansion featuring a white front porch with a profusion of fuchsia pink flowers. "Welcome to Magnolia Street. We're an exclusive bunch."

Adelia glanced at her son. His hands were tucked in his pockets. He was at ease. He withdrew his right hand and extended it to Margaret.

"Good afternoon, Christopher Franklin." He gestured to his mother, hand open, palm up in front of her, keeping eye contact with Margaret. "And this is my mother, Adelia Franklin. I assure you, Ms. Thurnwell, we bought this house because it is exclusive."

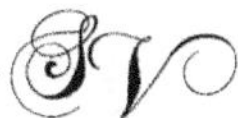

Adelia shot him a look with a slide of her eyes while faking a smile toward the abrupt woman standing in front of her. "Nice to meet you, I guess we're neighbors now."

Margaret shifted the tiny dog to the front and kissed the knot atop the creature's head. "Is that your car?" she directed the question to Chris.

"No," Chris stated.

The woman nodded. "I suppose it'll be parked in the garage, so there's that." She cuddled the squirming Yorkie with her cheek. "Luciano, where are your manners. Hush." She turned back to Adelia. "Where did you say you were from?"

"I didn't," Adelia assured, her tone taking on the professor vibe. The one that had authority with an air. "We arrived from New Hampshire."

Chris leaned against the emerald, green car. "Now that we've made your acquaintance, we'll be sure to let you know when there is a housewarming. For now, we are anxious to assess my dear mother's new abode." He pushed away from the car and motioned for his mother to take the lead before him toward the front step.

"Good day, Ms. Thurnwell. I do hope we see you again," Adelia chimed as she walked away.

Margaret coddled the yorkie and stepped back to the sidewalk. She stared at a parked golf cart in the distance, a woman of indeterminant age perched in the driver's seat.

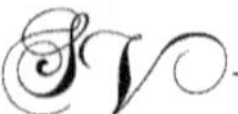

Once inside, Chris watched her from the foyer window. "What a strange woman."

"It's no different than starting a new job. Everyone's going to crane their necks to peek at the shiny new addition. There's obviously some sort of rivalry going on. Did you get a look at the glance exchange between Margaret and whoever was driving the golf cart?" Adelia shook her head watching Margaret and the yapping Yorkie through the window. "A chic replay of the Hatfield's vs. McCoy's."

"Whatever it is, stay clear of all of them. Until we can have a proper introduction with a housewarming, keep them at bay. You know full well how to play hardball. You were an ivy league bulldog," Chris chided.

Adelia laughed, "Me? I'm not the bulldog. You're the bulldog. Marking your territory and puffing your chest out. I like to think of myself as a poodle. Smart, beautiful . . . "

"And intent on drowning when you get soaking wet," Chris laughed. "Poodles drown unless their furs clipped."

"And bull dogs drool," Adelia retorted. "What the hell does this have to do with Ms. Thurnwell and the busy bodies?"

Chris grabbed a bottle of champagne off the white marble bar counter just off the foyer. "I don't know. But I love throwing around metaphors." He popped the cork and poured two glasses in a set of flutes that were beside the bottle.

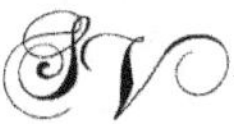

"When did you set this up?" she asked.

"I arranged for the housekeeper to have it ready for your first visit. Now, mom, come explore the grandeur of your new home." Chris put his arm out for Adelia. She held onto him and walked into the living room and saw a glass elevator with a large bouquet of pink roses. The living room featured mahogany floors with white satin striped wallpaper and a large white marble fireplace with a massive mahogany mantle.

"Christopher Franklin, this is beautiful. I can picture our Chippendale furniture in the middle on that emerald oriental rug. And the flowers, you didn't have to do that."

"No, I didn't. But they are from all four of us, ma. We love you and want the best for you. It's an act of appreciation. None of us want you to forget how beautiful life can be. There has been so much heartache, we want you to remember the little things. The small touches that made everyday special growing up, are what we are trying to give back to you." Chris led her to the elevator and pressed the panel. The door hissed open. "After you."

Adelia stepped inside the glass box of the elevator. "I don't know what to say. This can't be my home. It's more like a hotel or a museum. A white urn with long stemmed pink roses was tucked in the corner. She stood next to the urn as Chris entered the box beside her. He pressed the button for the second floor and the elevator obeyed without

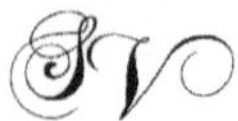

a sound. The door opened to a large empty room with long floor-to-ceiling windows facing the back yard.

"What is this room?" she asked.

"I was thinking it could be your studio. We haven't seen you pick up a brush in over two years," he said.

His mother smiled. "Has it really been that long?"

"Time gets away from us, steering us astray. I figure the passion you had all my life was still in there. Maybe you don't want to teach anymore, but I doubt you've given up on art. It is who you are. You spent thirty years teaching but what you love is painting. Art is as much a part of you as we are. And your art is part of our generational wealth. It's worth more than you will admit." Chris patted her arm. "Go check it out."

Adelia stepped into the large space. There were mahogany floors to match the downstairs, but on the far side of the room there was tile. A small sink and built-in counter were set beneath a long string of windows facing Magnolia Street. "I haven't worked with clay in several years, but that area would be perfect." She sighed, "I can picture my easel set up over there." She pointed to the windows facing the back. "My drawing table can go against the wall here, and maybe my pottery wheel will fit on the shelf by the sink. All my paints and brushes will have a spot on the built ins. Oh, Chris this is just what I needed." She took off to the next room. "Is this the master suite?"

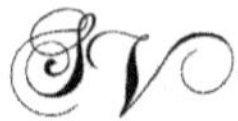

"It is," he called. "The movers will be here in about three days to set it up."

"I can just picture our, I mean your father's and my bed facing against the inner wall to allow me to see the front and back. What a spacious sitting room. Do the doors really open to a balcony?" She walked to the doors and opened the French doors. "Oh, this is lovely." Adelia stepped on to the balcony that looked out at Margaret's home and a good portion of Magnolia Street. "I'll have them set up the bistro set here."

The two returned to the bottom floor and made their way to the kitchen. It was a large open space with white and glass lit kitchen cabinets, polished black marble countertops, a hidden refrigerator, gourmet stove, and single serve coffeemaker. The mahogany floors flowed into terracotta for the kitchen. Large green potted palms adorned the corners on either side of the floor to ceiling windows. A wall of glass doors opened to an atrium with white wicker furniture and more green plants.

"Did you arrange for the plants and furniture, too?" Adelia didn't wait for him to answer. She swept her hand over the glistening surface. "This is some kitchen, Chris."

"Hopefully one you won't need to use. At least not often," he winked. "You have access to the finest dining available, and delivery from outside restaurants." He took their empty champagne glasses to the sink.

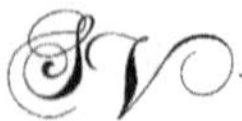

"I completely forgot; we have reservations for tonight. We should check in at Abby's, the bed and breakfast outside the gates. I'm getting hungry."

Chris escorted his mother from the kitchen back to the half-moon driveway where the car waited. He handed Adelia the key fob. "Care to drive?"

Adelia nodded as she slid in behind the wheel and drove them out of Savannah Valley's gate toward the bed and breakfast in the tiny town. It was a Victorian manor with an oak lined drive. A small pond with a fountain welcomed visitors. The wrap-around porch had cushioned wood swings, pitchers of lemonade, iced tea, and several glass domes with cookies, cupcakes, and candies. A large woman at least ten years Adelia's senior arose from a wooden rocker and met them on the steps.

"Good evening, may I hep you?" she said.

Adelia extended her hand. "Yes, my son and I booked the chalet for two nights. My name is Adelia Franklin."

"Oh, yes. Follow me." The woman opened the screen door. "I'm Rudy. Let's get you checked in. Now you wanted the private chalet." She was a jolly seeming woman, at least to Adelia. Her warm brown eyes, and gray hair framed her face. The manor had dark wood and large exposed beams. The furniture was soft, clean, and inviting.

"I hope the chalet is as beautiful as the main house," Adelia cooed.

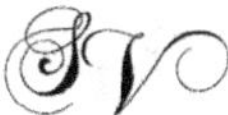

"Why thank you, darlin'." Rudy smiled. "It is my masterpiece."

Chris took the key and shook the woman's hand. "From the look of things on the porch, breakfast will be fantastic."

"You bet, scrambled eggs, creamy grits, fruit tarts, ham, homemade biscuits and red-eye gravy every day. Honey, you won't find a finer breakfast in all of Georgia." Rudy winked and swatted the counter. "Now you two get a move on. Do you need me to make dinner reservations in town?"

Chris smiled, "Thank you, but no. We have reservations at the Sky restaurant in Savannah Valley."

"I've heard of that. What you get here is home cooking at it's finest. But I don't do supper," she laughed. "Especially that kind of supper."

Adelia thanked the kind woman and led the way to the porch. Chris followed his mother. She was at ease outside the gates of Savannah Valley. Large homes and filled spaces with exposed wood and throw pillows warmed her heart. They got back in the car and drove to the location Rudy showed them on her hand-drawn map. As they approached the small chalet with its black roof and white clam shell siding, she glanced at Chris. "It's adorable. I could be very comfortable here."

"Agreed, but this is just for a few nights," Chris said.

Adelia parked in front of the chalet. The small porch

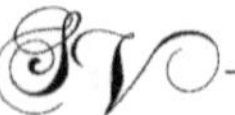

housed a red door that opened into a small living room. To the back there was a bedroom with a full-sized bed and across the way another door led to a smaller room with another full-sized bed. A large bathroom with a garden tub was situated between the rooms with a panel of windows that looked out on the back lot filled with pecan trees, peach trees, and bleeding-heart bushes. In the front there was a full kitchen and maple dining set.

"Mom, you take the larger room. I'm going to freshen up for dinner," Chris advised.

Adelia put her suitcase on the bed and laid the garment bag on a floral bench. She unzipped the canvas to reveal a Gucci pink sequined gown. The shoe box with a matching pair of low half-inch heels was in the car. Adelia often kept what she considered to be 'show' shoes in the car. It was easier to change into them at the venue or when nearing the end point. Tonight, she planned to slip them on at Sky. She had her everyday diamond earrings, took them off, and swapped them out for a more elaborate rose diamond drop set in white gold which matched the shimmer of silver in her hair. The earrings were part of a set that included a white gold bracelet and tear drop necklace, the last gift her husband gave her. She slipped into the dress, donned the jewels, and dug through her suitcase for the small make up bag. She used her liquid foundation, dark brown liner, and ebony mascara. She dabbed on a bit of shimmering rose lipstick and teased the front of her hair before securing the back with her grandmother's antique clip. She took one last look in the mirror, shocked to see the woman staring back at her. She remembered the last time she wore this outfit. It was for the annual alumni fundraiser—only a few days before the news came about her husband's cancer.

Chris donned his Armani suit and added a diamond studded tie clip.

The two exited the chalet and climbed into the emerald Mercedes. He gave Adelia the pass card for the entrance to Savannah Valley. Once she drove through the gate, Chris directed her to the tower where Sky was housed. The glass tower reflected the waning day light. The valet opened the doors for Adelia and Chris. She slipped her sequined shoes on while Chris went to her side, offering his arm. She took it and they went into the building, the doorman holding the gold framed door for the two guests. To the left they entered an all-glass elevator that went straight to the top floor of the tower. When the doors opened, the expansive restaurant unfurled before them. On the far side was a set of folding glass doors that were open to the roof top and setting sun on the horizon. In the middle was an ebony piano with a woman playing soft jazz.

A young man approached Adelia and Chris. "Good evening, my name is Arthur, and I will be your host. May I have the pleasure of learning the name of my guests?"

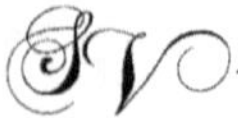

"Adelia Franklin and my son Christopher Franklin. May we have a seat outside?" A smile covered her face.

Chris smiled. "I knew you'd like it. How could you not love those colors?" He nodded in the direction of the horizon off in the distance.

"Right now, I'm taking in this polished black granite floor and black lined tabletops. It's fabulous," Adelia said. She followed Arthur to the outside dining area in the exposed roof top garden. The sun cast peach and pink streaks through the aqua blue backdrop. The mother and son took their seats as Arthur handed them their menus. Adelia glanced at the view and the community that spanned the full 360 degrees around them. Her eyes twinkled with unshed tears.

"Are you happy, mom?" Chris asked.

Adelia nodded, "Yes, Chris. I think I am."

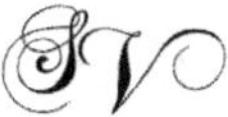

CHAPTER 3

Water Lilies

SV

Adelia sat in the black dining chair. She took the white linen napkin and folded it across her lap, after laying the silverware on the black tablecloth beside the white porcelain plate. Arthur motioned for a waiter to come to the table. Christopher picked up his menu. Adelia did the same.

The waiter approached the table and joined Arthur who stood with his hands behind his back. “Welcome. I’m Daryl and I’ll be your waiter this evening. May I start you off with a drink? You will find our exclusive wine inventory here.” He slid the black leather-bound booklet onto the table.

“I’ll just have water,” Adelia said.

“Sparkling, mineral, purified, or spring?” Daryl asked.

Adelia glanced at Chris, “Uh, spring.” She folded her lips.

“Imported or domestic?” Daryl offered.

Adelia smiled. “Imported, I guess.”

“And for you sir,” Daryl asked Chris.

“I’ll have a Perrier with orange twist.”

Daryl nodded to affirm, “Would you care to hear our specials this evening?”

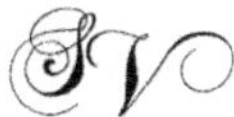

"Yes, please," Adelia answered. She straightened in her seat and tugged the napkin back into place.

Daryl pulled a slip of paper from his jacket's inner pocket. He followed with a pair of reading glasses and dropped the paper. "Oh, excuse me."

Arthur knelt to get the slip of paper at the same time Adelia bent to assist the waiter with his dilemma. Daryl also bent to grab the object. And in the attempt to show acts of kindness, Daryl's lip came in contact with the back of Adelia's head which had come up as she sought to retry her grab at the floor for which her reach was a tad too short. Arthur's head jerked back, as Daryl's, was on the decent. When Adelia's head hit Daryl's face, she ducked into Arthur's thus smacking her chin on the back of his barbered scalp. Adelia hollered as both men moaned in pain.

"I'm so sorry," she exclaimed.

Daryl bowed, "No, it was my fault. Please, allow me to grab your drink orders." He pulled his hand away from his lip to peek and Adelia saw the blood fill the cracked pink skin.

Arthur stood with his hand on the back of his head. "All is well, Mrs. Franklin. Daryl, we'll grab Silvia to assist in taking over until you're situated." He tried to smile. "I do apologize. Please excuse us."

"Oh, my goodness." A deep female voice rushed to Adelia's side. "Mrs. Franklin you're bleeding!" The woman grabbed a napkin from a nearby four top and handed it to

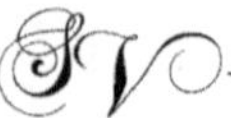

Adelia. “Come with me, darlin’. The ladies’ room is right over there.” The woman took Adelia’s arm and helped her to her feet. The napkin in her lap fell to the floor.

Chris jumped up, “I got it!”

“I’ll be right back, Chris,” Adelia said through her fingers.

“I’m so sorry, Mrs. Franklin. My name is Edith. I’m one of Savannah Valley’s owners.” The woman said. She opened the black lacquer door to the ladies’ room. The vanity set before the actual restroom had three gold and crème velvet stools, white marble tissue boxes, and motion sensor lights over the frameless mirrors. “Have a seat, I’ll bring you a wet paper towel.” The woman hurried to the sink area and brought back several paper towels.

“It’s fine, I’m fine,” Adelia assured. Her pride took a beating. She took a tissue from the vanity counter and dabbed at several blood drops on her the pink sequins of her dress and sighed.

Edith sat on the stool next to her. “What a way to make an introduction,” she laughed, a kind of laugh that one knows is more to break the ice. Adelia smiled and Edith continued. “I met your son during the initial interview process. He is a remarkable young man. You must be proud.”

Adelia nodded, “I am, thank you.”

“Well, he told me you are a connoisseur of fine art. Is

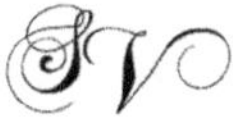

that right?" Edith asked, reaching for a folded newspaper in a leather wrapped box.

"I don't know about connoisseur, but I taught art history until my recent retirement," Adelia confirmed.

Edith slid the periodical across the vanity and pointed to the photo on the front. "This is our own publication, the *Savannah Valley Times*."

Adelia picked up the paper and stared at the photo. Her beloved neighbor, Margaret Thurnwell stood in a plunging V-neck Calvin Klein pantsuit with her arms crossed, smiling in front of what appeared to be a Monet. "That looks like a piece of Monet's *Water Lilies* collection."

Edith smiled. "Very good, it is in fact a Monet. We had a tremendous outpouring of interest to the article featuring the piece. And though we have a community filled with art collectors, we do not have," she sat back and crossed her legs, "correction, we did not have an expert in the field. As Christopher must have told you, Savannah Valley is a retirement community for the uber wealthy. We want the best there is and ensure those standards are not only met but maintained."

Adelia set the newspaper on the vanity. "I'm not certain I'm following you."

"Oh, I'm sorry. This is not how I hoped to approach you with the subject. But what's a ladies' room if not a bonding ground," she laughed, "unless we have a kitchen and brownies. But that's a story for another time."

Adelia smiled and blotted her sore lip. The bleeding wet the surface and she winced. "Sorry, it smarts." She glanced in the mirror and touched around the edges of the split with her pinky. "It was all in good humor." She slid the stool away from the vanity and left the outer room to wash her hands.

When she returned, Edith was holding the paper. "Come, I'll have Arthur grab a frozen peach daiquiri." Edith stood and slid the stool back in place. "Oh, I was asking if you'd like to write a weekly piece in the Arts section of the paper. We have our performing arts covered, but we have many interested parties wanting to stay in the loop with what's what in the fine art world."

"I'd like that," Adelia said, her cheeks flushing. "Let me get settled and I'll reach out to you or whomever is overseeing the articles."

"Wonderful," Edith said. "Christopher has my direct number. Put me in your contacts. I want you to head this up, because frankly you're the most qualified of our residents and you bring longevity. It's a win win." She held the door for the woman and followed her back to the table, waving to Arthur. "Peach daiquiri for my dear Mrs. Franklin." The young man made his way to the lavish mirrored bar in the center of the room. Edith turned back to Adelia,

“Look through the paper and let me know if you have any ideas to strengthen the Arts section. Oh, and there’s a concert by our very own Savannah Valley Chorale conducted by the Goddard Sampson. The theater group will also be performing in the new Arts Center, too.”

“Thank you for the opportunity,” Adelia said.

“You are welcome, my dear. Now, you should try the lobster thermidor with frisée salad. I had it earlier, and I must say, pure heaven.” She turned to Chris. “A pleasure to see you Mr. Franklin. I do hope you choose one of our exquisite steaks. The likeness will not be replicated in any establishment outside of Savannah Valley. Now, I must continue my rounds. Do enjoy.” Edith left the table waving to a two-top near the front of the restaurant. Two ladies sat waving back. The odd woman in the deep purple suit wove her way through the tables toward her other guests.

“Way to make an entrance, Mom,” Chris said, laughing. “Are you alright?”

Adelia folded her injured lip. “My pride’s hurt the most, but what can I say,” she shrugged. “At any rate, I landed a job.” She showed the paper to Chris. “I think it best if I attend both performances. It says Patricia Smithfield is the contact for theater tickets. Her number is listed here, and then there is one for Linda Foss for the concert. I wonder why there is no box office?”

“Whatever the reason, I’m certain that getting in

contact with these women will prove fruitful. Now, let's order." Chris picked up the menu and continued to scan over the steaks section.

Adelia didn't bother to read it over. "I'm sure I'll have plenty of time to learn the menu, I'm going with Edith's suggestion. I think a little lobster to celebrate my new endeavor is just what this doctor is ordering."

The two laughed and enjoyed the lavish plating of their dishes. Chris had a gold grade porterhouse while Adelia sopped up the rich brandied sauce pooled around her lobster. They sat beneath the open night sky and listened to the evening jazz. After their dishes were cleared, they left Sky and headed back to their chalet.

• • •

Adelia parked the car. When she opened the door the sound of serenading crickets and the distant croak of frogs surrounded them. The warm Savannah breeze stirred the leaves and weeping fronds of the majestic oaks and willows. Chris opened the door to the chalet and sat on the porch step.

"Waiting for me?" Adelia asked.

He leaned back on his palms. "Simply enjoying the new woman standing before me. It's been years since I've seen you just enjoy. Let me take a picture to send to Charlotte, Sam, and Michelle." Adelia obliged, spreading her arms toward the sky. Chris took the photo and sent it to his sisters.

"You know, you bought the house as an investment, correct? That is what you said." Adelia faced her son.

He scratched his head and patted the porch next to him. "It sounds like you have something specific you want to ask. Your Socratic methods aren't necessary. I'm an adult. If you have a question, just ask. I know your love is unconditional."

Adelia sat beside him on the porch and cupped his chin, meeting his eyes. "Is the house in your name?" She let go.

He sighed. "I'm an investment banker. I invest. Maybe I have a small interest in real estate investments that include you. And maybe the house was purchased via the company which may have you as an officer and thereby you are the owner of that house, and maybe have an account with a small bit of funds to equal those lovely neighbors around you."

"Wait, you asked me about becoming an officer for Franklin Inc. before your father passed. You made me the President, and if I remember correctly, you gave me control of all the assets." Adelia tapped Chris' arm. "So how does this work?"

"You are the sole shareholder, the assets of the company that include the house and bank account are yours. I've been investing for years. The house is yours, free and

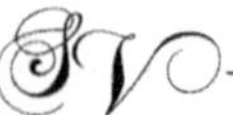

clear, no mortgage. It's all about you having a quality of life in retirement that you so richly deserve, mom. I know you and dad had a plan for the future, but things changed."

"That's an understatement. Even with all our saving over the years, in the end it evaporated. I never thought that could happen."

"Well, it does, and it did. But that is no longer a problem for you. Enjoy life. The truck will be here soon. The movers will set up all your belongings in whatever manner you wish. I've hired a housekeeping service to come three days a week, a gardener to come daily, and ten mil in the Savannah Valley Credit Union. Is there anything I missed?" Chris asked.

Adelia gasped, "Ten million dollars?"

Chris hugged her and swiped away the tears rolling down her cheeks.

She wrapped her arms around him. "Thank you, Chris. You are an amazing son."

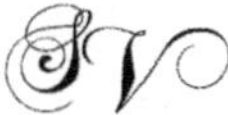

CHAPTER 4

STICKS & STONES

Four o'clock struck on the grandfather clock. Adelia was alone in Georgia for the first time. She'd slept through the night aided by her Melatonin with a chamomile chaser. Chris was safely back in New York and Charlotte video chatted to make sure she was tucked in bed, safe and sound. She relished her children's love. But guilt bore down and washed over her. She didn't want to burden them. They doted on her when Ted passed. The last thing she wanted was for them to feel responsible. She stood in the great white living room with her precious painting above the mantel.

The greenery that surrounded the house in the painting popped on the white wall and merged, as Adelia suspected it would, with the emerald rug. The mantel had to be ten feet long, a massive piece of carved mahogany wood with lyre endcaps. The fireplace itself was white marble with a low fire. The light from the crystal chandelier reflected off the shining surfaces.

She returned to the kitchen with its white surfaces and stainless-steel appliances. Her own touches of beeswax yellow candles and fruit bowl filled with green grapes, lemons, and pears added a splash of color. The cabinet doors

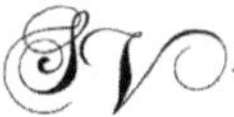

with glass panes let her see what was inside. Chris directed the movers to place her belongings in locations similar to where they were in her New Hampshire home, but also took her shopping to pick out some new pieces to complement her new life. She retrieved a teacup with a lavender stalk painted on the side.

Adelia chose an entire set with lavender clippings painted on the dishware. She loved Spanish lavender, bright pink azaleas, majestic oaks. Bright colors in a haven of green and white. She poured a cup of hot water and measured a ball of white tea with rose hips into a tea ball. The scent soothed her morning angst.

Her mind drifted back to move-in day. The golf cart from her first day at the house paused in front of her house again. Two women took pictures and drove away. That was just before the moving truck arrived. When the truck pulled up, they putted down the road.

The woman across the street, Margaret, sat on her porch with her little dog lunging on its leash. When the golf cart stopped, her neighbor whisked the dog into her arms and retreated into her house. Adelia wondered if the someone called to complain about her, but she couldn't imagine why.

"Chris," she had said. "Do you think she called those women?"

"For what? You haven't even moved in yet." Christopher

glanced toward Margaret's house. "If you suspect trouble, you have Edith's number. She's the owner. I'm sure she can address your issues. It pays to have friends in high places." He kissed Adelia's cheek. "Mom, you are the least of Savannah Valley's worries. Unless you go all Pink Panther with a plan to steal the baseball diamond or whatever they have kept under lock and key, you don't need to worry."

Adelia smiled. Still, she wasn't sure. Those women did not look friendly. Margaret disappeared anytime she looked her way. There was no comradery to be had on Magnolia Street—of that, Adelia was certain.

She came out of her reverie and sipped the tea. She took a pear from the fruit bowl and headed to the atrium off the kitchen. The lead-lined windows and white rattan furniture with overstuffed violet pillows seemed too nice to squish. She ran her hand over the fabric. It was tough, outdoorsy. A throw pillow on the chaise had a more inviting texture. A faux fur case and matching throw blanket. She insisted there be no real fur. It was a firm stand. Even in New Hampshire, she and Ted never had real fur.

Whenever she went shopping with the girls, they'd stop at the pet store in the mall. They would pet the chinchillas and rabbits. The cute little faces always evoked feelings of remorse in Adelia's gut. She could never understand how something so adorable could end up wrapped around someone's neck. She opted for faux no matter how she would be judged. Though during the holidays, she was delighted to find real leather jackets to be a harder find. Most of the local outlets carried faux leather as well. It made her heart swell, knowing that there was some semblance of a voice for the innocent.

When she finished her breakfast, she washed her cup and went to the foyer. It was sunny, warm, and the blue beckoned. She slipped on her sandals and opened the door. On the door mat was a picture of her and Christopher standing next to the Mercedes.

"What the hell is this supposed to mean?" she exclaimed. She stepped into the driveway and searched the street. There were no cars, carts, or pedestrians. "How long has this been here?" She sat on the top step and turned the photo over. The word Exclusive was written in large black letters.

The bright blue day turned to haze covered doldrums. The kind of melancholies women mistook for mild panic. When she found herself troubled by Ted's issues and their financial woes, she turned to the only thing that gave her an out, painting. She went back inside, closed the door, and stuck the picture in the side table drawer. Intent on recapturing the day's charms, she entered the glass elevator Chris had built in before they arrived. It took her to the second floor that she dedicated to her art. She kept blank canvases, easels, palettes, trays, and buckets with paint

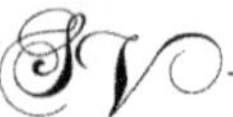

bottles on the tarp covered floor. She picked up a clean palette, a tool belt filled with brushes, and a carry case filled with tubes of acrylic paint. Grabbing an easel, she got back in the elevator intending to go outside to create. But the door would not close. She backed out of the glass enclosure and put the easel in first. The doors closed with the stand inside. She pressed the button for it to open and slid the case of paints, and her palette aside. The tool belt she secured on her waist, but the doors closed again. She slung the belt over her shoulder and pressed the button. When the door opened, she slipped inside, and let it close behind her. She managed to get the belt secured before she exited the box on the first floor.

Adelia took the paint and palette to the back garden door. She returned to the house for the easel and glanced at the elevator. "That thing is going to be the death of me," she muttered.

She trekked to the center of the yard. A flowering garden flanked the sides. A ceramic bench held up by cherubs seemed to capture her interest. She set the easel in front of a mass of white lilies and lilacs. The bench became a part of the scene. She took out the colors she needed and squeezed small amounts onto the tray.

"Crap, I forgot the water." She took off the tool belt, set the palette on the grass, and headed back into the house. She normally used an old rinsed out soup can to clean her

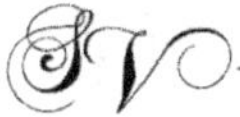

brushes, but Chris had bought her a proper plastic container with a jug to collect the dirty water. She grabbed them from beneath the kitchen sink and headed to her set up in the garden.

She covered the canvas in a layer of white gesso. As she studied the pink and purple dots on the lilies she thought of the photo. *What if I'm being watched?* she thought. There was a high white fence on the edge of her property. She scanned the edge along the line in front of her. *I'm being paranoid.* She continued to scan the line around the back and then turned around. The house was in the way of the other side.

Adelia left her canvas to dry. She wandered into the atrium and brought back her tea. There was a black wrought iron bistro set on the cream-colored patio brick in a sitting area surrounded by lilacs and honeysuckle. *I really wish Ted was here to see this.* "Damn that picture!" She hopped up from her seat and ran to the atrium to grab her phone. When she pulled up Chris's contact, she shot him a picture of the photo in the text and another of the reverse side.

Later that morning, while Adelia was busy working on the flowers' detail, she heard the front doorbell ring. She set the palette on the lawn and balanced the brush on the water cup. She'd been lost in her project and nature's beauty. The color splashes and delicate detail provided her an abundance of subject matter to recreate. In that moment she

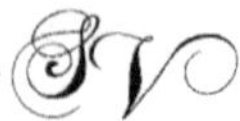

felt a kinship with Monet. His fascination with his water lily garden and backyard stream brought some of Adelia's favorite works into being.

She grabbed a rag from her tool belt and wiped her hands as she walked around the atrium to see who was in front of the house. *Why chance getting paint on the door-handle?* she reasoned with herself. Her gray yoga pants and white T-shirt were dotted with paint, both past and present. She had her hair pulled back in a low pony and donned a wide brimmed sun hat. It wasn't her best look, but she never painted in good clothes. It seemed wasteful. As she rounded the corner, she saw the two women from the golf cart.

Adelia froze.

"Mrs. Franklin," one of the women called.

"Yes," Adelia said.

The woman slid her sunglasses to the tip of her nose and looked down at Adelia's paint spattered attire. She frowned, creasing the skin around her lips. The skin tight and unforgiving. "I am Lisa Conway."

The shorter woman dressed in a white tennis dress and shoes smirked. "I'm Katherine Zimmerman. We are here to officially inform you of the decision to review your status in Savannah Valley. It has come to our attention that you in fact are a resident of a property not purchased by you. This home was purchased by a Mr. Christopher Franklin."

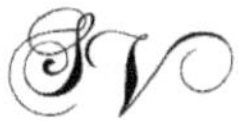

“Yes, that’s my son,” Adelia informed. “Is there a problem?”

Ms. Conway replied. “This house was purchased by a gentleman who is not a resident and does not meet the community guidelines for age restriction. The owner of this property is not of the retiring age of 55 or greater. The community is exclusive to a certain level of affluence and age requirements. We have brought the issue to the attention of the Savannah Valley Board and are providing you with a letter of intent.” The woman held a purple envelope out to Adelia.

Adelia stood her ground. “I don’t know who you are, but you can take your letter with you on your way off my property. You are not welcome here.”

“Funny you should say that,” Katherine hissed. “That’s how we feel about you.”

Lisa Conway put the envelope on the doormat and the two women walked back to their golf cart. Margaret emerged from her white double doors in time to see the women putting down the road.

Adelia’s phone buzzed in her tool belt. It was a text from Chris. “I’ll call you tonight at ten. Love you.” She went back to the garden, gathered her things, and put them in the elevator to take upstairs to what she hoped would be her studio. The thought of losing this beautiful dream home sickened her, so she left them in the glass enclosure

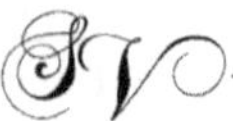

and headed into the house to shower and change. She put on a periwinkle dress and sandals. It was a new gift from Chris at one of the stores next to the bed and breakfast. She enjoyed having him to talk to in the mornings while they waited for the moving truck. At that moment she missed him more than ever. She thought about calling her daughters, but she knew they were unhappy with her decision to begin with. The last thing she wanted to hear was an 'I told you so.'

She opened the front door and stared at the purple envelope.

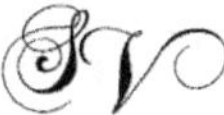

CHAPTER 5

MARGARET

Adelia stood propped against the white limestone pillar. It was one of the nine that graced the front of her antebellum home. She held the lavender envelope in her hand, the scent was one of perfume and flowers. The letter was crumpled in the palm of her hand. Margaret sat across the street in her white wicker rocking chair. She raised her hand to Adelia. After her morning tea and unpleasant exchange when she discovered the owners of the threatening letter tucked into her door mat, she was in no mood for Ms. High and Mighty. She turned her back to her neighbor. Tears stung her eyes.

Chris wanted me to be happy. If I were to call him, what would he say? she thought. When Chris left for New York, he made her promise she'd contact him if need be. She recalled their conversation.

"Mom, you're a curator. A woman with a mission, a duty. These people will eat you for breakfast if you don't put on your game face and show them who Adelia Franklin is. But don't hesitate to call, it's not easy being the odd duck in a pond of swans."

"I'll be fine, Chris. The art world is cutthroat. There isn't much I haven't seen."

His frown acted as a warning. "Maybe so, but these aren't the type of people who graced Dartmouth's gallery halls. These are the people who demand wings be built to honor their name, and then eat the art for emphasis."

She remembered cuffing his arm and laughing. That was when she protested the Mercedes S class car. *Maybe I should have taken him up on the Maserati. But that would have been ridiculous.* She was lost in thought when tiny paws scratched at her bare calves. Her periwinkle sundress let the slight tan bit of leg show above the matching sandals. She glanced down, to see Margaret's Yorkshire terrier at her feet.

"I want to ask you to lunch," the familiar and unwelcome voice called from the middle of her circular driveway. "I've requested finger sandwiches and fig cakes. I assume you like tea?"

Adelia stepped around the dancing dog. "Margaret? What?"

"Lunch. In my garden. You are free, aren't you?" The tart woman asked.

"I am, but." Adelia stuttered, "I, uh, I don't understand." She held the purple envelope in front of her.

Margaret approached and took the crumpled note, opened it, and read. "Rubbish." She folded the paper and handed it back to Adelia. "Bring it, we'll burn it." She stooped to pick up the canine. "He didn't scratch you, did he? Luciano is a spirited one." She turned away from Adelia and followed the driveway back to the street. Peering over her shoulder, she smiled. "Do you like mint juleps?"

"But I'm not dressed properly."

"Pish posh. You're fine. Now come along."

Adelia hurried her pace. The other woman waited for her before crossing to her own driveway. The lemon pudding house filled the lawn beyond the cobblestone drive. An enormous fountain with a stone koi spitting water stood in the center of a marble basin. When they passed the structure, Adelia noticed several large koi fish swimming in the clear pool. The porch was painted white with matching wicker furniture. A sofa, swing, two rockers, and a dining set filled the one corner. Margaret stepped onto the porch. A young man held the door open motioning for her to enter.

"The garden is set, ma'am," he said. He reminded Adelia of her own son. Broad and tall. But this gentleman had thick red hair pulled back into a bun.

"Thank you, Clay." Margaret patted the boy's shoulder. "This is my nephew. He's my personal chef when he visits. He's been all over the world taking lessons from the greatest culinary masters. This is my neighbor, Adelia Franklin."

The boy nodded at Adelia. "Pleasure to meet you."

"You as well." She folded her hands in front of her. The dress was sans pockets. A short maxi. It didn't allow for awkward encounters. And to say the day had been filled with them was an understatement. Adelia refrained from straining to look at the halls of paintings with gold-leaf frames. She thought she saw the Monet from the picture of Margaret in the *Savannah Valley Times*.

"Is that a Monet?" Adelia asked.

Margaret turned toward the painting; her lips parted into a soft smile. The smooth skin around her mouth creased on one side. "Are you a fan?"

"I am. I wrote my dissertation on Monet's influence on modernism. May I have a look?"

"Absolutely," Margaret affirmed. Her shoulders relaxed with a sigh. "I have a passion for fine art. It seems you do as well."

Adelia laughed, "I'm a retired art history professor. Art was, is, my life."

Margaret smiled and asked what Adelia assumed to be a trivial question but knew her answer was not to be taken lightly. "Where did you teach?"

"Dartmouth," Adelia confirmed. "I was the department chair."

"Oh," Margaret exclaimed. "Really. Then you and I may have more in common than I thought."

"What do you mean?"

"Let's just say, I am a fine art connoisseur. I savor long strolls through the world's greatest museums. The Louvre, London's galleries, Tokyo. You name it. I hired a procurer to acquire a Monet because his piece *The Water Lily Pond* moved me to tears. I was transformed into his early century garden." She laughed, a deep throaty laugh, it is in fact how I met my husband."

The women paused in front of the painting. Adelia's interest was now in the woman standing, posed, beside her. "Was he an artist?"

Margaret shook her head, "Oh, goodness no. He was the curator I hired to find my piece. His passion for early impressionist painters mingled with my own. When I saw his raw excitement for the piece, I asked him to dinner. Not just any dinner though," she winked. "We went to the black-tie gala at the Met."

"Your first date was at the Metropolitan Museum of Art? In Manhattan?" Adelia asked. She'd visited the museum a handful of times and organized trips through Student Activities to get her students to view art in a new way. She wanted to show them that there were no limitations when it came to art. "You must have a penchant for fashion then, too."

Margaret turned to face Adelia full on. "Come. Let's eat." She strode to a wall of white, paned-glass doors. They opened to a courtyard adorned with glass mosaic inlay and a walkway. A tower of finger sandwiches, tea cakes, and fresh fruits sat on a pink veined marble top table tucked in the garden's corner beneath a weeping wisteria tree.

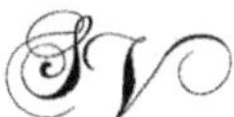

Margaret motioned for her to sit in one of the oversized white wrought iron chairs adorned with pinstriped green on green cushions.

Adelia noticed the woman liked color. She kept within the scheme, no contrasts. It echoed the woman's personality, at least what she was learning. She liked things just so. "This is lovely, Margaret." Adelia sat, taking in the blooming flowers that stretched across the three-acre expanse.

"Thank you. Call me Marge. Margaret is so formal. We're friends now. I hope you like bourbon. Pappy Van Winkle is as good as it gets, and I grow the mint myself." She sat in the opposite chair and sipped the iced beverage from the silver julep cup.

Adelia had never tasted a mint julep. As was her nature, and the experience she accrued over her career, she deducted that anything with sugar was swallowable. Follow the lead in the situation. She mimicked Margaret's sip. "Oooh, that's nice." She was pleasantly surprised by the refreshing sweetness. "That is delicious."

Margaret threw her head back laughing. "Honey, that's why you never settle for bottom shelf." She settled back with a chocolate dipped fig. "Mel, my late husband, loved his bourbon. I couldn't get behind it until we ran a horse in the Kentucky Derby. It wasn't my kind of event, until I attended. The excitement increased ten-fold after three of these."

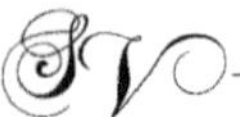

"You had a horse in the Kentucky Derby?" Adelia asked, taking a cucumber sandwich. She settled back and nibbled the corner of the crustless triangle. "I feel boring. My Ted and I traveled to a few places in Europe, but mainly ventured in our backyard, so to speak. We were content." She popped the rest of her sandwich in her mouth and sipped the julep.

Margaret leaned forward and put her hand on Adelia's knee. "I'm jealous." She sat back hard, her torso shaken by the motion. "Adelia, you had love. A family. My Mel was a late love. I was forty-eight when we met. He was sixty. My first husband was a schmuck. We annulled the marriage after just six months. I was in art school."

Adelia sat up to listen and take a mini chocolate bundt cake.

Margaret also took a bundt, holding it in her hand waving it around as she explained. "He told me I would die penniless. There was no money in art and my degree wasn't real. I lost my purpose for school. I questioned my future and saw the mounting debt behind the scenes. I let him into my head before my sister talked me into dumping him. I dropped out of the art program. It took a decade for me to return, but not before I learned about fashion. I discovered my knack for style in California, after I transplanted there in the seventies via my VW Beetle bus. It was all bell bottoms and daisy wreaths. A guy my friend met in

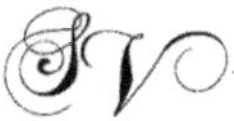

our hometown of Newark, was heading west. We decided to hitch a ride. To become part of this," she wiggled the cake and plopped it in a napkin on her lap. "Hippy movement. Peace and love. I was sold."

Clay stepped in with a fondue pot with creamy white cheese and a tray of steamed vegetables and lightly toasted bread cubes. Margaret leaned forward and picked up a long silver fork before skewering a broccoli floret. "When I got to Cali, I met a guy. He liked my look, a pair of jeans I'd created from a pair of hand me downs, and the jewel lined seams. He offered me ten million for the idea and a job as a designer. I wound up finishing my degree at UCLA while working. When I graduated, I started my own company designing clothes for high profile events. I've since expanded to all corners of the fashion industry with over three hundred companies. And every chance I get, I put my name in some publication that will make its way to Newark to show that ex-husband of mine that he can kiss my rich you know what." She sipped the julep and maneuvered the cheese covered vegetable into her mouth.

Adelia folded her lips, swallowing a giggle. This tough woman was a fighter. Adelia had a newfound respect for her prospective friend. "That's very impressive."

"So is what you do. Look, I have a vault of fine art. I didn't create them. I didn't study them. I don't even have anyone to show them to," Margaret said. "When Mel died three years after our wedding, I was crushed. He was my best friend. A fellow art lover. It's hard to connect with people in that way unless they share your passion. It's all about the passion, Adelia. Which brings me to your letter."

"Oh, yeah. I forgot, for a moment. I'm not like you or the others. Obviously, my son has money. This is his gift to me. But I don't belong here. The note says so." Adelia pulled the crumpled letter from beneath her leg, where she had tucked it.

"Nonsense," Margaret hissed. "Who are they anyway? A self-created committee. I certainly wasn't notified of any such entity. Let them tell me you don't belong. And who exactly is on this committee. Before you go to their so-called hearing, you need to gather a backing—an army. It's politics on the most pompous level. Beat them at their own game. Not Christopher. You. You don't gain respect by backing down."

Adelia bit her cake. "I don't like confrontation."

"Then honey, you need a new middle name." Margaret glared at the sandwich tower. "Uh, why are they always so tiny. I'm freakin' hungry." She put one of each sandwich on her plate for a total of eight. "Let's do dinner tonight. I have some friends I'd like you to meet. They're a couple of firecrackers."

With that, Adelia agreed to join her in her Garia four-seater cart.

• • •

The cream-colored golf cart with leather seats, and mini refrigerator was quiet and smooth. Margaret took off down Magnolia Street away from the community center where their dinner reservation awaited.

"We'll swing by Josie's house before stopping to gather Tanny. Our reservation is at eight and it's three thirty now." Margaret eased on the accelerator. The little car seemed to float over the asphalt road.

Adelia took in the mansions set back from the roadway. "I have to ask; how do you manage three hundred companies?"

"Delegation and outsourcing. After my first billion, I realized I needed to shrink my circle. I have two accounting firms and six attorneys on retainer in Manhattan."

"Billion?" Adelia whispered.

"Yup." Margaret sped up, glancing at Adelia. "When you make money, you invest. Some runs from you screaming, and some comes back to make you very, very wealthy. I learned a long time ago that the bricks you lay early in life build a strong foundation for the future." She pulled into a blacktopped driveway outlined in stone. The house at the end was a scant smaller than Margaret's. It was a stone mansion with large ebony doors and black iron work. A woman dressed in a silver evening gown and white gloves

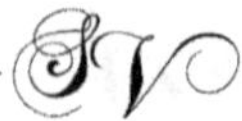

waved frantically at the two women as they drove through the porte-cochere. Margaret beeped twice and parked. “And that Adelia, is Josie.”

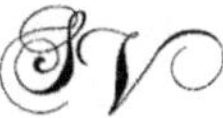

CHAPTER 6
JOSIE

Josie's sequined silver form descended the external stone staircase, her silk gloved hands glided over the black iron railing. Adelia likened it to Scarlet O'Hara in the movie *Gone with the Wind.* Her stride appeared flawless, but Adelia knew practice and repetition created the illusion before her. Margaret parked the Garia golf car in one of the glass enclosed garage openings within the porte-cochere.

"Marge!" Josie cooed from the bottom step. She waited for Margaret and Adelia to come to her. "I see you've brought a friend." She jutted out a white gloved hand to Adelia. "Josephine Rolland."

Adelia put her own hand out, but the woman squeezed her fingers instead of shaking it. It wasn't a business shake but a chic greeting. The kind Adelia observed on television and in old movies. "Adelia Franklin, nice to meet you."

"Any friend of Marge is a friend of mine. Welcome." The woman went to Margaret, "Lovely to see you."

"As always," Margaret returned, and they kissed cheeks.

"So, what brings you my way so early, Marge?" Josie asked, turning to go back up the long stone stairway. The two women followed her.

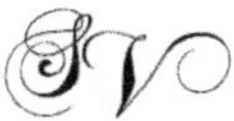

“The Rat Pack,” Margaret snorted.

Josie glanced over her shoulder and shook her head. “What are they up to this time?”

Margaret held her hand out to Adelia who handed the crinkly folded letter to her new friend. “Here.” Margaret handed the letter to Josie.

Josie paused, opened the letter, and read. Her lips pulled taught; her forehead almost wrinkled as she forced her thin brows to furrow. The woman was a sight, to Adelia. Her auburn pixie cut framed her petite features. Big brown eyes scanned the note. She handed the lavender paper back to Adelia and turned back to Margaret. “I thought it might be serious since you didn’t bring Luciano. I know Penelope would have loved a visit.”

“Penelope is Josie’s, teacup poodle. She’s such a love,” Margaret said to Adelia. “Luciano is with my nephew. My plan was to gather you and head to Tanny’s. Our new neighbor needs friends in high places.” Margaret clasped Adelia’s arm.

Adelia smiled but thought again, *Christopher Franklin what did you get me into?* She followed Josie to the landing with Margaret still attached to her arm. The woman she thought was her nemesis was now gathering a posse to fight for her honor. She entered the manor through a set of French Doors in the middle of an expansive wall of white paned windows. The white marble floors with gold grout drew her attention. *I didn't know gold grout was a thing?* she thought. She shifted her focus on a set of three white velvet sofas with oversized pink fluffy throw pillows showcased in the middle of the room on a black oriental rug. Large pink orchids filled vases around the room. A crystal chandelier hung from the cathedral ceiling off an exposed beam. She folded her arms over her chest, afraid of tainting the white.

A glass two tier coffee table sat in the middle of the three sofas. A tray with fresh grapes, strawberries, and a pitcher of fruit infused water sat in the middle with three tall glasses. Each had a sphere of clear ice.

"Please, sit. I was trying on my gown for the concert tomorrow evening. Do make yourselves comfortable while I go change," Josie said as she whisked herself away through a set of dark walnut doors.

Margaret flopped on one of the sofas and pulled a pillow into her lap. "Well, that explains the gown. Not that I wouldn't put it past her to float around in a gown or two for no reason. She lives to enjoy. We could take a lesson from her. It doesn't matter if she's going for a walk with Penelope or having pizza with Tanny and I on a Tuesday, that woman loves to live it up."

Adelia nodded. "No harm in enjoying life."

Margaret laughed, popped a grape in her mouth and poured a glass of water. A blueberry splashed leaving a

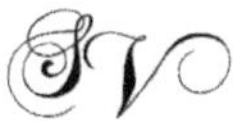

droplet of water on the table. She wiped it with her pinky and sat back. “Want some? It could be a while. Then again, she was already primped so, maybe just a quick change. Whatever. Have a glass.” She handed the water to Adelia and then poured a glass for herself. “So, before your day was rudely interrupted, did you have plans?”

“I was painting,” Adelia shrugged. “I lost the motivation and left it for another day. Maybe when this is dealt with, I can focus. Finding my muse requires letting my mind wander free, taking in the beauty Savannah Valley offers. I have to appreciate it to let show on the canvas.” She sipped and peered at Margaret, “The letter has filled me with angst.”

“Nonsense,” Josie called from the back of the room. She’d entered through a different door. “The bitties, and that’s what they are . . . don’t have to be old and bitter. You can be old and love life. They are the kind of women that get joy out of sucking the life from others. Soul suckers, that’s what they are. Old bitter soul suckers.” She grabbed a strawberry and curled up on the middle couch. Her olive-green onesie had three quarter sleeves with black leather cuffs. They matched the black around the ankles and the corset belt. She slipped off her gold sandals to tuck her feet beneath her. “Did I hear you say, you were painting? As in art?”

“I did,” Adelia affirmed. “I was an art history professor.”

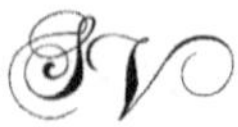

"At Dartmouth," Margaret informed. "Never sell yourself short here, honey. Own it."

Adelia nodded.

Josie savored the strawberry and tucked it into her cheek, "Art history. I'd love to show you my collection." She hopped up and slipped her sandals back on, holding her hand out to Adelia. "Come, we ride the lift down, I keep them in the vault." She took Adelia's hand and pulled her through the door from where she'd entered. Margaret followed.

The three stood in the middle of a black ironwork elevator. Margaret glanced at Josie and tapped Adelia's shoulder. "Josie's quite animated."

"Hey, I'm right here," Josie laughed. She squeezed Adelia's shoulders. "I don't like bullies, and that's exactly what they are. They have no authority in Savannah Valley and are a thorn in the Rich Widows' keisters. I'm not sure how you made your money, maybe it was art, or your son, or what not. But the fact is, it doesn't matter. Those women have lost the joy. Life is filled with pleasures of all sizes. I have money, more than I know what to do with."

"I'm sorry I'm causing such a stir," Adelia whispered.

Josie waved her off. "After my husband passed away, I was lost. That was when I was in my fifties. It took me a decade to learn that I had a life to live. One that was my own. When he died, he left 700 million and a company

I sold for one point five billion. Do you know how lonely that is?" Josie frowned. "I decided to indulge myself. We'd spent our time together building our business, just for him to have a heart attack and not get to enjoy what he made. I vowed not to work myself to death."

Adelia offered Josie a reassuring smile. "I lost my husband this past year. He also had a heart attack. It's tough rediscovering yourself."

Josie pressed her forehead to Adelia's, "We made tape. Tape. Let that sink in. Everyday, my husband dealt with orders, recalls, shipment issues. When he died, I wanted no part of it. It turned my stomach just thinking about the manufacturing and board meetings. That's why I sold it. My daughter moved to Hong Kong. The last thing I, or she, wanted was to deal with the whole mess. She has a life of her own, a son and husband. What was I to do?"

Adelia couldn't believe she was hearing her own story retold by someone else. But it was too soon to share. She heeded her own warning to her children, *Loose lips sink ships, Adelia,* she reminded herself. She was in the company of people she often admired for investing in the arts. These were the people who made contributions for libraries, museum wings, and made the art programs within community youth centers. They were the kind of people Adelia never thought she would rub shoulders with. Most often she remained silent and offered a pleasant smile with

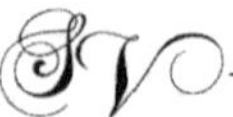

a handshake at her speaking events. In Savannah Valley, standing in a mansion that trumped her own, she stood in awe as she had all those years in her professional career. She would maintain her composure and focus on the small talk. Give just enough, which was always her way. "I've been through that. That's why I'm here."

"And these old rats want to try and dampen your sunny days," Josie said as they exited the elevator into a stone lined hall below ground. "Every day, I will wear, do, and eat what I want. If I wake up wanting a brownie for breakfast, I'm going to have it. How old are you, Adelia?"

"Fifty-five," she said.

"Oh, for heaven's sake, you've got a lifetime ahead of you. Follow me and put that letter out of your mind." Josie opened the vault with a facial scan and thumb print. The door opened and the motion sensor light flicked on.

Original works in gold leafed and thick wood frames leaned against the walls. Adelia counted twenty-three pieces. Josie handed her a pair of white gloves, which Adelia slipped on before wandering to the collection furthest back. She peeked behind each to take in what she saw. Rembrandt, Monet, Van Gogh, and Warhol made her heart race. She ran her hand over one that took her breath away. "Is this a Raphael?" she asked.

"It is. I acquired it at an auction in London back in eighties," she affirmed. Josie and Margaret stood beside Adelia.

“The young women in his paintings always seem to have a smile. Unsure if it is contentment, happiness, or melancholy. But I love the way he captures their innocence as they cuddle their children. It takes you back in time. Looking at the clothes, the dress draped over her shoulder. The color blue. Where did they get the fabric? Who made it? Dyed it? How many miles did the garments travel?” Adelia sighed, “I bet the clothes and the water pitcher have their own story to tell. Everyone focuses on the main subject, but they forget. The details and pieces in the background were a part of their lives. It was pre–Industrial Revolution. There is so much more than color and facial expressions within these pieces.” She moved on to another stack.

Josie looked at Margaret. “She has a gift.”

Margaret nodded. “This collection is impressive. I should show you my own one day.”

“Absolutely. And Adelia, you will have to tell us all about them. Your excitement is intriguing.”

“My son always says investments in real estate and artwork are the cornerstones to generational wealth. They grow in value and can be used, enjoyed, or sold when the time is right.”

Margaret tapped her index finger to her lips. “But that’s what your son says. What do you believe?”

“Oh, for me art is about the joy it brings. I focus on the composition, the technique, its place in history.” She

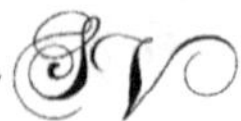

glanced at both women. "Honestly, investing in art was never in my mind—nor my means."

"I think we are all going to learn about art from new perspectives from each other," Margaret said with a satisfied grin.

Josie folded her arms. "I think we need to head over to Tanny's. We'll take my car since she's in the condo on the other side of the community."

"Sounds good," Margaret said.

Adelia was admiring a French landscape painting by Camille Pissarro. "This is exquisite. Did you know he was known as the 'dean of Impressionist painters'?"

Margaret and Josie shared a knowing smile. "Time to go, Adelia. We're taking you to meet Tanny. You're going to love her penthouse."

"And we'll take my Aston," Josie added.

Penthouse and a James Bond car? Adelia thought, *this day gets more and more interesting.*

"We'll never fit!" Margaret exclaimed.

Josie batted her eyes at her friend, "Not my precious, the newest model. It's a five door four-seater."

The three women left the vault to close behind them and headed to the underground garage. Josie led the way followed by Adelia and then Margaret.

Josie peered over her shoulder at her neighbors. "We are three women on a mission. One that involves taking

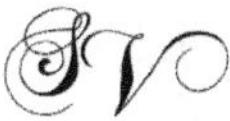

down the Rat Pack. I believe Bond said it best, 'Once is happenstance. Twice is coincidence. Three times is enemy action.'"

Margaret laughed, "Quoting *Goldfinger* now, are we?"

"We're three women climbing in an Aston Martin, Marge. Who else would I quote?"

Adelia laughed and joined the women in the silver sleek car still clutching the lavender letter in her white gloved hands. She sat back in the red leather seat and whispered to the sliver of sky she glimpsed from the window, "You'd never believe this, Ted."

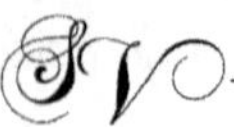

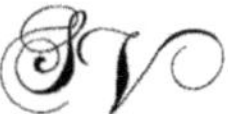

CHAPTER 7

TANNY

Josie pulled up to the glass front of the lobby. The valet wore the Savannah Valley uniform of red jacket with brass buttons, black trousers, and white gloves. Adelia noticed she was still wearing the gloves from Josie's vault and slipped them off. She still had no pockets or purse. She folded them and put her letter on top of them when she exited the Aston Martin.

The attendant opened the door and pointed the way to the white marble concierge counter. A woman chewing gum and blowing tiny bubbles greeted them. "Good evening, how may I help you?"

Before the women could speak, a female voice tutted from the lobby behind them. "Joooossiiie, Maarge."

Margaret bumped Adelia with her elbow and swirled around to meet the woman calling her name. "Adelia, meet Doctor Tanny Willias." The woman's smiling sun-kissed face beamed. Her silver hair was swept into a loose bun held in place by a wooden clip that matched her olive-green sundress and leather sandals. Margaret went to her with both hands outstretched.

Tanny clasped her hands, grinning. They exchanged air kisses and then Josie took her turn. Adelia stood back with the letter and the gloves clasped in front of her. Tanny

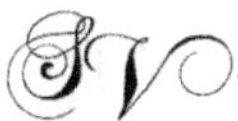

glanced at Adelia. "Call me your friend, Mrs. Franklin. I do not take kindly to people putting down another based-on perceptions. Perceptions of any kind fosters malice." She held her hand out to Adelia.

Adelia faltered, "How did you know my . . . "

Tanny stepped forward. "If these two haven't told you already, there are no secrets in Savannah Valley. At least not among us. Welcome!" She gestured before walking toward the open door.

Adelia obliged and followed the woman into the gold and marble elevator. Tanny scanned her key card and the doors closed behind Margaret and Josie. Adelia turned the letter over to expose the gloves in her hands. "I apologize. In the excitement, I forgot to remove my gloves back at your place, Josie."

Josie waved her hand, "No bother, I toss them in the trash. No contaminants allowed near my precious pieces. Just discard them when we get to Tanny's."

The elevator whispered to a stop. The brass doors opened to the tenth-floor penthouse. Floor to ceiling windows faced the expansive 18-hole golf course. Massive forest green velvet drapes accented the ends and pooled on the black marble floor. Silk cream upholstered armchairs and settees seemed lost in the massive salon. White marble walls with gold veins and cherry wood curios showcased mounted ancient pottery pieces, urns, and masks.

Adelia folded her lips to keep from gasping. The space was warm, museum-like, and filled with natural colors. Greens, creams, soft yellows, and browns. A bar to the right of the elevator had a black marble countertop. A handful of jade and white porcelain pieces were on display in front of the ceiling high mirrored back drop. A small glass front refrigerator was filled with bottled water.

"It's gorgeous out today. Join me on the terrace," Tanny took Adelia's gloves and dropped them on a table as she moved across the room. She stepped through a glass door hidden in the middle of the wall of glass. The women followed her. Several junipers and potted ferns filled the corners. A wrought iron bistro set for four had oversized cushions with watercolor lemons. "Sit, let's discuss the unpleasantries before dinner. Let's not allow the embittered musings of others thwart that." Tanny sat in one of the chairs. A young woman in black-on-black outfit brought four bottles of water and had a basket of cherries that she set in the middle of the table. "Thank you, Kelly." The young woman disappeared back inside the penthouse.

Adelia set the envelope on the table before she tucked her dress, taking a seat next to her newest ally. Margaret and Josie sat next to each other on the settee.

Tanny pointed at the lavender envelope. "Is that the communication?"

Adelia nodded. Her heart was in her throat. She was

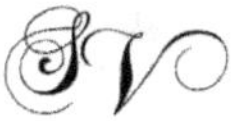

used to formality and airs, but that was when she was able to disappear into the background. It was the first time in her life she had to remain in the foreground. As a professor and lecturer, she knew how to command the forums and stages, but in her personal life she was reserved. She used years of practiced poise to cover her angst as she did sitting in Margaret's garden, Josie's salon, and now on Tanny's terrace. "It is," she responded, sliding the envelope to the woman beside her.

Tanny pulled a pair of reading glasses from her dress pocket and reached for the letter. She unfolded the wrinkled paper and read aloud.

Attention: Mrs. Adelia Franklin
This letter is to inform you of our, The Savannah Valley Rules and Regulations Committee, intent to bring before the Board of Directors, an order of eviction on the grounds that the property and residence located at 114 Magnolia St. is in breach of the bylaws set in place by the founding members. The property has been occupied by you, the non-title holder for a property purchased by Franklin Inc., and, according to our records, is an entity registered by one Theodore Christopher Franklin. The age restriction in the Bylaws states:
NO member shall be less than five and fifty years of age at date of purchase. After pursuing the matter through the employment of one private investigator,

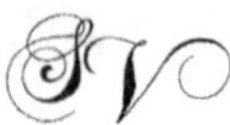

Mr. Samuel Sanchez, it has been determined that the resident within this manor has knowingly and fraudulently acquired the afore mentioned lot.
We ask that you vacate the premises, or further action will be required.

Regards,

The Rules and Regulation Committee,
Lisa Conway, Committee Chair
Katherine Zimmerman, Secretary

Tanny removed her glasses, tucked them in the bosom of her blouse, and tossed the letter on the table. "May I be honest, Adelia?"

Adelia nodded.

"The bylaws in any housing organization are administered prior to the sale of property. At the time of closing the purchaser must sign a form indicating the understanding of the bylaws and their intent to follow them. Before purchasing your property, you must have known about the bylaws, and someone had to sign the document or there would not have been a sale."

Adelia's heart sank. She hadn't been part of the sale. But Christopher told her she owned the property outright, free, and clear. "I wasn't available for the sale, but . . . " she held her tongue. *I know better than to disclose personal information. I don't know if I can trust these women yet.*

Margaret squinted at Adelia then stared at Tanny. "Perhaps the best course of action is to start with your background so that she feels as though there is an alliance surrounding her. Her apprehension speaks volumes."

"Agreed," Tanny said. She settled into her seat and folded her hands across her lap. "Adelia, I am Dr. Tanny Willias, MD. I was born in the Nunavut territory. My motivation for studying medicine lay within the limitations set on my family when my grandmother needed a lung transplant. We relocated to Ontario where I finished school and went on to study medicine with a focus on pulmonology."

Adelia picked up a glass, sipping the cool sparkling liquid. Although she enjoyed sparkling water, she wasn't expecting it. She stifled a cough as she attempted to choke in silence. "Excuse me," she said.

Tanny gave her a reassuring smile. "Adelia, I own a pharmaceutical company and have practiced medicine for over fifty years. I read people. Right now, you appear out of your element. But there is no right element. As an art history lecturer and professor, you hold a respectable position in your corner of the globe. Is anything in the letter false, to the best of your knowledge?"

Adelia shook her head, "I own the house with no obligations. Yes, my son purchased the house for me via the company, but I am the sole proprietor of Franklin, Inc."

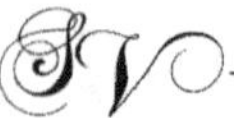

Tanny shot a glance to Josie, "We need to contact the board."

"Actually, I just happen to have Edith's number in my contacts. I was waiting to call because," Adelia interjected.

"Because you don't want to rock the boat as a new resident," Margaret finished. "Honestly, I thought the bitties were ogling your Mercedes. They have a thing for bright, shiny objects." She swigged her own water. "Dial Edith, we'll let her know what the Rat Pack is up to; she'll handle it. They need to be soothed."

Tanny laughed, "You need a housewarming party. A big soiree. What are your plans for the week?"

Adelia opened her mouth, then closed it. "I don't have any. Just the concert tomorrow." She grabbed the letter on the table, folded it, and slid it back into the envelope.

Josie's chair screeched across the terrace floor as she pushed away from the table. "Tomorrow everyone who's worth knowing will be at that concert. We'll make a guest list during dinner, and I'll order the invitations through the print shop in town. We'll contact the Savannah Valley catering service. We'll hand out the invitations tomorrow during your introductions." Josie brushed her hands over her jumpsuit. "Well, come on ladies, we have to change for our dinner reservations. I'll drop Adelia off at her house."

Josie added, "Margaret, I'll bring you to mine to grab the Garia." She strode through the terrace doors.

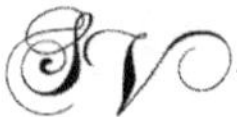

"We'll see you tonight. Thank you, Tanny," Margaret said as she stood to follow Josie.

"You two run along. I'd like to speak with Adelia a little longer." Tanny turned to Adelia, "If you don't mind."

Adelia nodded. "That would be lovely." She sighed and leaned back against the chairs.

"Then I guess we'll see you ladies at dinner. I'm famished." Margaret waved to Josie, "Wait up. I'm coming." She disappeared inside the salon and Adelia could hear the two chattering and planning. Their voices waned.

Tanny leaned toward Adelia. "Take a deep breath and put this nonsense out of your mind. Tell me about you. What brought Adelia Franklin to Savannah Valley?"

Adelia tucked the light blue fabric of her sundress beneath her thighs. *What am I supposed to say? That I lost my husband thrusting me into a whirlwind of foreclosure at the same time becoming a member of the millionaire's club?* The reality of the situation before was that she didn't know these three women. They were strangers and up until that afternoon, she'd have bet money on Margaret being her nemesis. But Tanny was a doctor, she wouldn't be so easily swayed from her reserved actions, Adelia knew that. "I hesitate, Dr. Willias."

"Because you don't know me?" Tanny said.

"It is not my intention to offend, but rather absorb and observe. I am not confident here at Savannah Valley, and that puts me in an uncomfortable position," Adelia explained. She crossed her ankles, regaining her old self. The one prior to driving Ted to chemotherapy treatments, prior to playing patient advocate, and prior to the grieving widow.

Adelia spent the next few minutes giving Tanny the condensed version of her life at Dartmouth, her husband's illness, and her son's plan for her retirement. "I'm still finding my footing, but the ground so far has been a bit wobbly," she confessed.

Tanny put her hand out to Adelia. "Take all the time you need. Know that you are not alone. Many residents have lost the loves of their lives. My husband lives here with me. He's out on the course, as he is every day. Tomorrow he'll be at the concert, but he knows this is my dinner with the girls."

Adelia took her hand, adding a light squeeze. "I appreciate your understanding."

The doctor stood pulling Adelia with her. "Give me a few minutes to change for dinner and then I'll take you home. Margaret and Josie plan to wait for us at Marge's. We're taking one of the complimentary limos. We always request the pink one for our girls' night out."

Adelia laughed deep and free for the first time since leaving New Hampshire. The warmth Tanny offered balanced out the eccentricities her neighbors exuded. *Dinner*

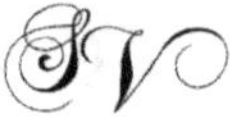

with friends. Do I know how not to be alone? "It sounds fun, I'm looking forward to it."

• • •

The pink Rolls Royce limo pulled into Margaret's half-moon driveway. The four women were dressed and ready for dinner. Adelia chose a black Calvin Klein pantsuit. Margaret changed into a mauve lace coverlet over matching silk gown while Josie wore a red backless gown with single shoulder strap and diamond necklace. Tanny sported a white sweater dress with wide tan leather belt and red Louis Vuitton's.

The chauffeur opened the door for the women and closed it after Adelia who chose to enter last. She hadn't been in a limo since her daughter's wedding. The three friends poured champagne and had a glass waiting for Adelia. Margaret held two bottles up for her to decide.

"Alcohol or non?"

"Non, for now. Thank you. I'll have wine with dinner though." Adelia accepted the glass from Margaret.

The limo took the women through the streets of Savannah Valley and pulled into the valet area at Sky. The chauffeur opened the door for the women. The doorman motioned for them to enter the building.

Adelia scanned the black marble floors, wood paneled walls, and paintings. "I was here with my son for dinner

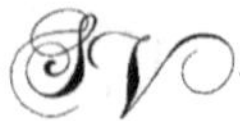

before I moved in. It was quite overwhelming. Everything is simply beautiful."

Josie still had her champagne glass and raised it to Adelia, "Correction, nothing here is simple. It is exquisite!"

Margaret put her arm around Adelia, "I'd say it was the champagne talking but she chose non-alcoholic, too."

"Hey, again, I'm right here," Josie pouted.

Margaret winked, "And that's why I said it."

Tanny pulled Adelia from Margaret's hold. "Dinner is never dull." She inserted herself between Adelia and Margaret and looped her arm through theirs. "I thought you were famished?"

"Honey, I am. But we need to paint a smile on our own Mona Lisa." Margaret nodded in Adelia's direction, then stepped into the elevator. "No sad faces. Oh, I wanted to bring home a filet for Luciano. Adelia, did you know Sky has a pet menu? I didn't notice a critter during your arrival, but for future reference. Let's just say, my precious boy just loves the parboiled salmon. The pet chef is the cat's meow."

"Reer," Josie scratched the air. "Penelope's a pescatarian and our personal chef Michael has her covered."

"Josie has a personal chef for the few days she eats at home with Penelope. Personally, I think she keeps him around as part of the décor," Margaret teased.

Tanny looked out at the art center as the glass elevator

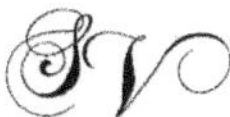

floated to the tenth floor. “Adelia, in case I forget, make sure you sit with us tomorrow for the concert.”

Josie tapped Tanny’s arm, “Like there’s a choice. We’re handing out her invitations.”

The host Arthur greeted the four women as the elevator doors slid open. A light evening drizzle created a blue gray haze over the rolling green meadows visible in the distance, in the dining area where Adelia and Christopher had dined only a few nights prior. The gracious host motioned for Adelia and her possible new friends to a table tucked in the left corner in view of the pianist and bar.

Adelia raised her finger, “Excuse me, but would you all mind terribly if we were to dine over there?” She pointed toward the enclosed outdoor dining area.

“The windowed section in the rain?” Josie asked.

“If you wouldn’t mind. I do love the rain and we’re well protected,” Adelia said. She fished her phone out of her suit jacket pocket, scrolling while following her entourage to their new seating assignment. Arthur pulled the chair from the table for Adelia, but she bypassed him standing before the floor to ceiling window. Margaret, Josie, and Tanny stepped up behind her. Margaret rubbed her shoulder. “I apologize,” Adelia held her phone up for them to see the image. “Are any of you familiar with John Frederick Kensett?” She glanced at the four onlookers; each shook their heads to indicate the negative.

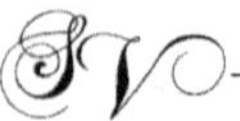

"John Frederick Kensett, *White Mountains.*" She points to the view behind her, "This is remarkable. If you look at this painting, you will notice his luminous style. A style that minimalizes the visibility of brush strokes. The entirety of the work is as if there is a haze of drizzling rain. Although the subject is that of my native New England, the resemblance is uncanny. The gray wash over the landscape and mist rising from the bright green grasses is breathtaking." She turned back to the view. "There is movement captured in all his paintings. Snapshots of stillness, a glimpse of life at a glance. In moments, this too will be lost without capture."

Arthur pulled his phone from his pocket and took a photo. "May I text this to Ms. Edith with a rendition of your words, Mrs. Franklin? This would be wonderful for next month's newsletter."

Adelia blinked, awed by the young man's expressed interest. "Of course, my goodness, I didn't expect to interrupt our dinner." She fussed to turn the phone off and make her way to her chair.

Josie put her hand on Adelia's arm. "That was beautiful."

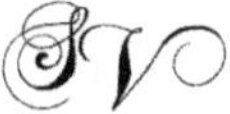

CHAPTER 8

PROPOSAL

"The guest list for your shindig mustn't be limited. Perhaps all-inclusive. There are only what, a few hundred residents? I'm sure half will decline," Margaret informed Adelia of the protocol. "A last-minute gathering such as yours will most assuredly bring the scorn of the Rat Pack." She smiled a sort of tight-lipped grin that grew to show her perfectly white teeth.

Josie raised a single manicured brow. "You know Ruby, Edith, Patricia, Goddard, and a handful of others are huge art collectors. We need to word the invitations in a way that markets Adelia's talents and expertise. Respect starts with the introduction."

"Ladies, neither of you stopped to consider Adelia's take on the potential invasion of her home by hundreds of strangers," Tanny interjected. "Adelia, what are your thoughts?"

Adelia swirled the glass of wine before taking a sip and setting it down. She pushed her poached salmon through the dill sauce smeared on her plate then resting the fork on the side. Sighing, she answered. "Honestly, I miss art being in my life. I was blown away by Josie's vault and to learn that there are other residents that are collectors of the same magnitude. It honestly blows me away." She picked up her fork again and took a full bite of salmon and covered her lips with the napkin. "I think a housewarming may be the way for me to meet like-minded individuals. I was asked to write an article in the arts section of the *Savannah Valley Times* and perhaps some of them would like to be highlighted."

"I would love to be your first," Josie hummed. "Margaret's already had her spotlight." She pursed her lips at Margaret.

Margaret perked up, rolling her shoulders back, striking a pose. "What? I'm photogenic."

Tanny and Adelia laughed. The wine warmed Adelia to the evening and the new friends she had earlier considered out of her league. The enormous mansions, lavish décor, and ease with which the women lived, and accepted their lifestyles overwhelmed her. Tanny seemed to be the one that resonated with what was comfortable.

Adelia did have dealings through her art history days where she was invited into homes of wealthy patrons, though she did not create friendships with these individuals. The relationships and experiences taught her to hide her shock. But those instances never gave her privy to those outside the art world. The people who did not hide their eccentricities. Her colleagues had different faces, the ones that kept a professional side that carried through and into

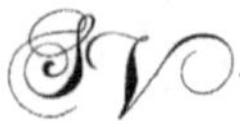

all aspects of life. There was an expected way to speak—a proper face to present and proper dress. One always had self-control in the presence of others. In meeting those women earlier in the day, Adelia found herself questioning, *who is it I want to be?*

"Ladies, I hope all is to your liking this evening," a familiar female voice caught Adelia's attention.

"Edith, I trust Arthur's text reached you promptly," Tanny said.

"It did," Edith said.

Adelia put the wine glass back on the table. A thought crossed her mind as she remembered her conversation during her first dinner at Sky. "Regarding the text and our previous discussion, Edith; I'd like to look at the empty room in the Art Center before tomorrow's concert. This evening if possible."

Edith took out her phone. "I'll contact security and be sure you have access when you finish here." The woman glanced at Tanny, Margaret, and Josie. "What has the three of you smirking so?"

Margaret straightened in her chair. "A little extermination of a few community rats. That's all."

Josie laughed full and hearty, "Please, they had the nerve to threaten our dear Adelia with an eviction."

"Eviction?" Edith gasped. "Whatever for?"

"They believe she purchased her property under false

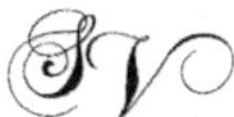

pretenses. They claim age requirement was fraudulent because of her son's involvement of the purchase," Josie elaborated. "With a housewarming invitation signed, Adelia Franklin, D.F.A., Franklin Inc, Owner, proprietor, the two will scurry back to their Brie-loving holes."

"Hey, don't insult the Brie," Margaret chided.

Tanny shook her head, "Insult it all you want unless it's smothered in chutney. Then we can talk." She sipped her Perrier. "Adelia's still finding her way and the truth is those women are making it difficult. She needs a plan that will showcase who she is. I'm not so sure a housewarming is up her alley. Some people have reservations about opening their homes to the public, no matter how much money they have." She glanced at the woman of the hour, "Adelia, what are you thinking? What do you want us to do?"

Adelia folded her lips and fiddled with the black cloth napkin in her lap. *Do I dare disclose what I want?* She glanced toward the rolling hills shrouded under the shadow of night. The truth was, Tanny pegged it right. She didn't want a house filled with strangers. She liked the privacy and tranquility of her new home. It was her shiny new hide away. She put on her managerial façade and turned to Edith, "It's a bold request, but you have an art center with a theater and concert hall. Would you consider opening a gallery? One that I would very much love to curate. I

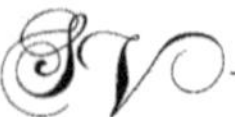

have a proposal that I believe would benefit the residents of Savannah Valley." She let out a wavering breath.

Josie thrust her hands in the air. "Oh, no way. Ladies, forget the housewarming. Adelia deserves a gala."

Margaret clapped. "Yes, a gallery opening with a gala, and I'll offer my Monet, providing security is at it's highest."

"Absolutely," Edith assured. "Write up a proposal; I'll bring it to my co-owners." She put her hand on the back of Adelia's chair, "This sounds fabulous. And to think you can literally say it was created through blood, sweat, and tears." She winked at Adelia as a reminder of the waiter mishap.

The women finished their post-dinner cocktails. Arthur greeted them at the elevator and held the door open. Edith disappeared to join another group when the four women decided to venture to the art center. The young man pressed the ground floor button and backed away.

"He's so cute," Josie kidded in the elevator.

Margaret rolled her eyes, "Josephine. No cougar action with our waiter." She put her hands on her hips.

Tanny smirked at Adelia, "I don't know about you, but I'm no cougar. I'm a panther all the way, baby."

"Oh, so dangerous. I like it," Josie teased. She led the posse outside of the Sky Tower lobby to the sidewalk where she pointed at the art center. "There she is."

The modern glass structure, comprised of large forward-slanting cubes, glimmered at the end of the roadway.

"Come on. Let's walk," she encouraged. The fluorescent interior had a single entrance where two security officers waited for their arrival. Adelia approached the walkway toward the large building taking note of the empty promising space in front of the building. She imagined a metal structure, one that moved with the wind. During her career she befriended two artists who created free standing pieces that connected physics and illusion.

Tanny, Margaret and Josie followed her lead to the entrance, trailed by the pink limo which parked discreetly at the curb. Adelia had no idea who contacted the driver, but it made her chuckle. "I feel like an art thief."

"Come on Inspector Clouseau," Josie teased.

Margaret overheard her statement, slipped off her high heels and tiptoed toward Adelia while humming the theme song to the *Pink Panther* movie, "Ba dum, ba dum, ba dum ba dum ba dum, ba dum ba duuuuudadadum."

Tanny fished around in her evening bag and pulled out a set of gold folding opera glasses that she substituted for a monocle. She joined Margaret holding the glasses to her eyes, singing along.

Josie rushed to Adelia's side and took her arm. "We need pink satin jackets with Pink Panthers outlined in Swarovski crystals on the backs."

Adelia let go and laughed. She accepted the comradery surrounding her. It felt good and real. She kept her guard up, but let the outlandish week envelope her, raising her spirits higher than they'd been in over two years. She and her three cohorts entered the center. Motion lights illuminated the lobby in front of the theater hall. A security officer led them to a large open space that spanned two stories. A white marble stairwell led to the upper level. Adelia climbed the stairs envisioning the placement of pieces she imagined remained hostage in dark vaults within Savannah Valley. She found a map of the building by an emergency exit door to study the layout and whispered to herself, "This place has to be at least 30,000 square feet." She decided to write up the proposal first thing in the morning. It was already clear in her mind.

• • •

A beaming ray of sun forced Adelia awake at just before nine. Determined to put her plan into action, she grabbed a bottle of room temperature water from her nightstand drinking the full eight ounces on her way to the kitchen to start her day. The proposal template was saved on her laptop from years of writing requests. She had grant templates too. *I'd forgotten that part of my life*, she realized. "I was a true believer in myself. That quality of life should increase so that dependence on anyone or anything wasn't even an option. Planning was supposed to take care of that," she boasted to the blinking cursor on her laptop screen. "It's about time I put my mantra back on the mantel."

Adelia's fingers flew over the keys as she found familiar words and phrases to express her desire. An exhibition showcasing private collections. Increased security, round the clock guards, and a controlled environment to house the works. Her sense of self returned through the completed proposal based on a template she used during her career. It was straight forward since the space was already there. She just needed the other owners to allocate her position as curator to the art gallery.

The night before she stayed awake until well after midnight sketching designs for the layout. She wanted free standing walls and a private room for secure cases. She researched security teams and determined to defer the reference gathering to the Savannah Valley Chief Security Officer and the owners. She included those plans in the proposal. After breaking for a cup of Oolong tea, she went back to the document, editing before sending it off to the email address Edith had texted her. "There's no turning back now," she hummed.

In scrolling through her text messages, she realized Christopher had not answered her message from the prior afternoon. He was supposed to get back to her after ten and here it was the next day. "Chris is more punctual than I am," she said to the phone. Instead of contacting him again, she decided to give her son until later that evening.

The concert was set to start at seven. Adelia was invited

to dinner at Margaret's since the woman's nephew was there for another day. Josie declined as did Tanny. Truth was, Marge did not give Adelia a choice. She gave her a time and told her to arrive before five because they had to leave at least thirty minutes to prepare for the night's outing. Since Edith hadn't contacted her, Adelia decided to put off any invitations for her gala. It seemed like a far-fetched idea to begin with, so it didn't affect her as much as she thought it would.

Dressed in a white Brunello Cuccinelli double breasted suit, Adelia left her house in time to see the pink golf cart putt by. She waved at the two frowning women and continuing to the lemon pudding manor. Margaret was on her porch with Luciano in her arms. He had a plastic cone around his tiny neck.

Margaret waddled off the white step in a Ralph Lauren black tight-fitting gown with large red rose blotches covering fifty percent of the surface. "Luciano had a reaction to the new cologne I bought. His backside looks like he sat on a fire ants' nest." She kissed the little muzzle growling at her affections. "That's my boy. Who's mamma's boy? You are," she cooed. The Yorkie showed his fangs while his tongue licked over his nose with ferocious sounds emanating from his throat.

Adelia backed up several steps. "He seems angry."

"Oh, he's just a cutie when he's all bothered," Margaret

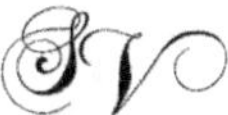

continued. She led the way inside while Luciano screeched his discontent.

Adelia stayed back in case the little wild thing broke loose. She loved dogs and animals. It wasn't until Ted became ill that she lived without a canine companion. Their German Sheppard passed from old age several months after her husband's diagnosis. They decided it wasn't wise to bring in an animal who would require so much attention when Ted needed it the most. But they both missed the companionship of a four-legged friend. It was their plan to adopt the week before Ted's heart attack. They'd made an appointment at the local shelter. Since then, Adelia put the idea from her mind. But seeing Margaret with Luciano, and then Josie talking about Penelope, the idea of having a tiny companion was inviting.

Margaret's nephew brought two plates to the patio table where Adelia joined her for a midday nibble the day before. "I omitted garlic, onion, fish, and eggs because you'll be greeting people this evening. The first course is a carrot cinnamon salad with fresh fig, to followed by a butternut bisque. For the entrée, I've prepared grilled lamb chop with fresh mint, and roasted beets."

Adelia glanced at the carrot salad. The grated vegetable and fruit was molded into a cylinder. The young chef stood back with his hands folded. "I looks lovely," she said.

Margaret beat her to the tasting. She scooped a bit of

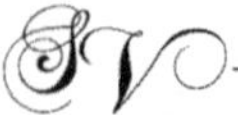

fig with the orange shreds and put her napkin over her lips. "Simply divine."

Adelia took a bit and savored the flavors that married as she chewed. "This is delicious."

He bowed, "Appreciated. I'll bring your next course."

The two women finished their meal while the young man watched. Adelia fought the urge to invite him to join. In her home, everyone ate together. It was awkward.

"It's almost time to leave," Margaret informed. "I'll introduce you to Goddard but he's quiet and will disappear for the night if we don't catch him early. He's a doll, but too serious."

Adelia sipped her Chardonnay, "I heard you mention him before, is that *the* Goddard Sampson, the composer?"

"The one and only," Margaret affirmed. "Since he took over the choir, concert attendance has filled the theater to capacity."

Adelia gulped the rest of her wine. "Then I expect he has an excellent collection waiting in the midst."

• • •

Josie waved at Margaret and Adelia from her black Navigator. She pulled into the driveway in time for the women to climb inside thearmored vehicle. "Tanny's already there with her husband. She texted and said Goddard and Gill want to talk to Adelia before going back to the green room."

Margaret chose the front seat leaving Adelia to slide into the back. The two women wore flowing loose gowns while Josie chose the gold sequined evening gown she modeled the day before. “It’s all glitz and glam tonight, Adelia. You ready? Words out—you’re a popular lady.”

“Why me?” Adelia asked.

“Because art is a very lucrative business. It’s a cutthroat industry, and a little birdy told a few friends about you. An artist is one thing, a curator is another.” Margaret swigged a bottle of B12 and tucked it back in her evening bag.

Josie tsked her, “You’d have more energy if you ate more vegetables. A multivitamin once a day and I’m the picture of vibrance.” She raised her brow at Margaret. “Didn’t you two see today’s paper? There’s an article about Adelia.” She pulled a copy of the paper from between the seat and console. “Here,” she said, handing to Margaret.

Margaret read the article aloud, “Savannah Valley welcomes Adelia Franklin, Ph.D. to Magnolia Street. She brings with her experience procuring, curating, and lecturing on Art History. Before retirement Franklin was the department Chair at Dartmouth University, served on the Art History council in Concord, New Hampshire, was a guest lecturer at Princeton, Middlebury, New York University, and other well-known venues. Franklin has been named the curator of Savannah Valley’s first art gallery,and the columnist for the Arts section in the weekend edition

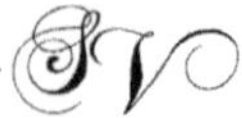

of the *Savannah Valley Times*." The woman turned to face Adelia.

"It was a lifetime ago. I'm different; life's different," Adelia stated, her voice soft.

The attendants at the theater approached Josie's Navigator as she put the car in park. Two young men opened the doors on each side of the car. After Margaret, they opened Adelia's. A valet climbed into the driver seat and drove away before Adelia had her crème and gold silk shawl over her shoulders.

Tanny rushed to meet her with an older man in a black suit and another that Adelia thought looked at least a decade younger. "Adelia, I'd like you to meet Goddard Sampson, and Gill Berm. They're performing tonight, so the greetings will have to be quick."

Goddard stepped forward extending his hand. His white hair was combed back, shaped around his ears. A fresh barber cut Adelia noticed. His face was smooth and clean shaven. "Good evening, Dr. Franklin. It is a pleasure. I must return backstage before the show. However, I would like to discuss several pieces in my penthouse that I would consider lending."

Adelia shook his hand, "A pleasure to meet you Mr. Sampson, I'm a huge fan. And thank you."

"Wonderful," he pulled a business card from his suit pocket. "Call me and we'll discuss the details. Enjoy the show." The quiet man slipped inside the theater doors leaving the growing audience members.

Murmurs and animated voices filled the lobby. Gill put his hand out to Adelia. "I must go as well but I brought a picture of my newest acquisition. It's a white relief by Ben Nicholson." He pulled up a picture on his phone and displaying the image to Adelia. "It is being packaged as we speak. Botan House will deliver the piece on Friday; at which time I plan to place the gem in my study above my Steinway."

Adelia took the phone from Gill. Her smile faded. "Mr. Gill, did you say you purchased this from Botan?"

"I did," the man affirmed.

"And it was authenticated? I assume the piece's provenance was questioned," she said. She enlarged the image, inspecting the signature in the lower right corner.

Gill took his phone from Adelia. "What are you suggesting?"

"I am not suggesting, but telling you, Mr. Berm. This work is not a Nicholson. He was a British artist who not only signed his work on the reverse side but dated and titled them. The picture you showed to me has a signature on the front and should never have passed authentication. The provenance is fallible." Adelia rested her hand on the devastated man's arm. The realization of her words played in his expression. "Mr. Berm, if you give me the name of

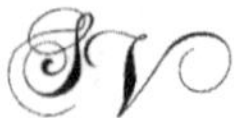

your procurer, I'll contact them tomorrow morning and discuss the terms of your sale."

Gill stammered. "I—what? It's a fake?"

Margaret squeezed the man's slacken shoulder. "A reputable authenticator would have spotted it at a moment's glance. We are lucky to have our own. If Adelia says it is so, I would take advantage of her services, Gill."

"I second that," Tanny added. "It may come as a blow to one's ego, and I believe it teaches us the value of a true artist. The works are held in the highest regard and many wish to profit from their talents."

Josie put her hands on her hips, shaking her head. "I don't know what you're waiting for. Give Adelia the word and she'll be on it. If there is one thing I've learned in our acquaintance, it's that this woman is the real deal, Gill."

The man flipped the contacts on the phone screen and pulled up the number for his procurer at Botan House and showed it to Adelia. "I paid over two million for this rubbish," he whispered, voice hoarse as he visibly struggled to keep his composure.

"I promise you, Mr. Berm, Gill, I will get your money refunded. It is unfortunate, but these houses are aware of frauds floating around. My mantra is if it looks too good to be true, question it until all red flags are resolved." Adelia put the number in her contacts and made a small note in her memo application with Gill's information and the

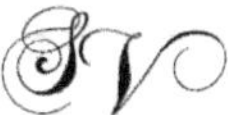

fraudulent Nicholson's photo. "Got it. Now, you have a performance to give. I look forward to hearing you."

The man stared at her as if in awe. She knew her art and the look from many who were blown away by her knowledge. In her younger years it filled her with pride. But as Adelia aged, she learned there was a purpose behind the learning. Beyond the appreciation of art. It was why she chose to go back for her doctorate in her late thirties. It wasn't so much the prestige, that was a given. Instead, she wanted to dive into those dark nooks and crannies of the art world. The ones that exposed exactly what Gill needed. She felt needed.

The women took their seats and the lights flickered as the crowd filed into the auditorium. Goddard Sampson was seated at a black Steinway center stage. The chorale lined the walls of the auditorium holding white candles. The master behind the piano stroked the keys filling the space with a haunting introduction and then, a hundred and one voices hummed Rachmaninoff's *Bogoroditse Devo* as they filled the stage on black risers.

Tears welled in Adelia's eyes. She hadn't heard a performance like that since the St. Petersburg Choir performed in Manhattan. Her arms broke out in goosebumps with the haunting melody that played into the melancholy she fought after discovering the fraud.

• • •

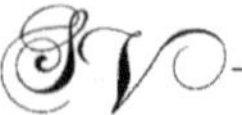

The next morning, Adelia woke early just as light was filling the sky. She enjoyed watching the sun rise through the colorful flora in her yard. It was time to fight for Gill. She readied herself for the day in the event of a video call, determined to bring whoever questioned her judgment to their knees. The glass elevator's doors had remained open. She stepped in, grateful the box whispered to a halt on the first floor where her attendant for the day was already in the foyer watering the house plants.

"Good morning," Adelia chimed as she hurried to the kitchen to grab a lime seltzer from the mini fridge.

She dialed the number to Gill's procurer.

"Bon matin, Botan House, Lawrence speaking."

"Good morning, Lawrence. This is Dr. Adelia Franklin. I'm representing Mr. Gilbert Berm regarding a recent purchase. I believe he is your client," Adelia started.

"Ah, yes. How may I assist Mr. Berm?" Lawrence asked.

Adelia frowned into the phone. "I am questioning the provenance of the Nicholson relief my client purchased last Wednesday. Can you tell me who was the authenticator?"

Lawrence gasped into the phone, "It was I, Dr. Franklin. I assure you the authenticity is without regard. The provenance checked out and the piece is in excellent condition. Mr. Berm was the highest bid."

"Let me be clear," Adelia said, air in her voice went back to her days speaking with colleagues at Dartmouth

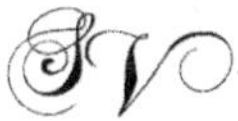

and with fellows at Harvard and Yale. "It is a fraud. A novice procurer knows the masters whose notoriety stands with not marking their works from the front. You have failed to see a signature on the lower right-hand corner. I will email Mr. Berm's formal request for immediate refund on the full amount paid and urge you to notify the FBI. There is no question. Botan House has at least one fake in its inventory."

"That accusation is unacceptable, Dr. Franklin. I am certain the piece is in fact a Nicholson. I am unpacking the piece at present." Adelia could hear the rustling packaging in the background. "Here it is. Yes, the piece is signed on the lower right-hand corner." The phone went silent. "Oh, no. Nicholson signed on the reverse. There is nothing." Another moment and the man's phone hit the floor. "Mickey!" he yelled.

Adelia heard the fumbling for the phone before Lawrence returned. "Please assure Mr. Berm a refund will be issued at once. Have a good day, Dr. Franklin." Before he clicked off again, she heard him calling for Mickey again. She assumed it was the owner but was satisfied knowing she thwarted scheme and fulfilled her promise to Gill.

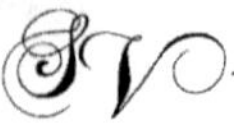

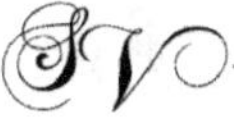

CHAPTER 9

STATUS 'NO'

Adelia sipped her gingerbread latte at The Garden of Evil restaurant. Just another of nine five-star places to dine in Savannah. It's sister restaurant, The Garden of Good touted to the longevity of life. It's twin, Evil, promised the absence of leafy greens. The restaurant was a stark contrast to Sky. The amber and brown tones, warmed Adelia through. Chocolate scones, raspberry tarts, and a year-round Christmas beverage list piqued her interest. Tanny appeared at the door and waved. She joined her new friend for breakfast. It was an unexpected invitation, but one Adelia was happy to have. "I'm so glad I ran into you. I'm nervous about the committee meeting on Thursday."

Tanny nibbled the edge of her Nutella toast. "Oh dear," she licked her lips and glanced at the Rat Pack that was entering the front door.

"Oh no. I wanted to get away from Savannah Valley for a few hours. What are they doing here?"

"We should invite them to join us." She didn't wait for Adelia to agree before waving her hand in the air, calling to Katherine and Lisa. "Good morning, ladies!"

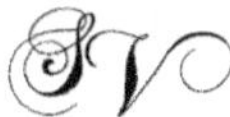

The two women grimaced at the woman vying for their attention. Lisa waved, “Good morning, Dr. Tanny.”

Tanny pushed away from the table and went to the condemnatory duo. Adelia sat with her hands folded in her lap, her foie gras and rye crisps sat abandoned on the red plate with a single flaming trident painted in the middle. Tanny put her hand behind her back motioning for Adelia to join her. Adelia did not.

Katherine shifted her weight from one foot to the other. It was clear to Adelia that the woman did not want to be there either. She also figured the leader of the pack was the feisty Lisa who dragged her friend through the game of petty pittances. Lisa walked toward their table and Katherine followed.

“Come, sit,” Tanny said.

“Oh, we couldn’t intrude,” Lisa said, glancing at Adelia.

Tanny pointed to the two empty chairs, “No, I insist.”

Katherine frowned at Lisa; her orange crush lips stressed her opposition. Her friend and counterpart shrugged and followed the woman who had drawn unwanted attention their way. They each slid a wooden chair from the table and sat on the edge of their seats.

“Well, thank you for inviting us this morning,” Lisa said.

“Oh, it was nothing,” Tanny replied. “But I will admit that I had reason.”

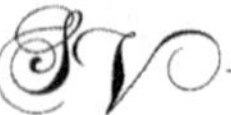

Katherine puckered her lips and flopped back in her chair. “I knew it.”

Adelia shifted uneasily but chose to remain silent, waiting to see what was about to transpire.

Tanny smiled the kind of smile that showed empathy. It caused Lisa to slide back in her chair and wave to the waiter. “One vanilla soy latte with Guatemalan dark roast and stevia.”

He acknowledged her with a nod.

“Same,” Katherine added.

Again, the waiter nodded.

Lisa took the red napkin from the table and folded it on her lap, “There is no beating around the bush, Tanny. We all know what this is about.”

Adelia sipped her latte, unsure of what was unfolding. Tanny patted her knee then faced Lisa with full eye contact. “I don’t want either of you to come off looking a fool. I read your letter to Mrs. Franklin and must urge you to pull the issue from the committee’s agenda.”

“We can’t do that,” Lisa said.

“For vanity’s sake you must,” Tanny insisted.

“We did our research, the owner of the property does not . . . ”

“Your research was fallible. Invalid, incomplete, and elementary,” Tanny argued. “The truth is that Adelia is the sole proprietor of Franklin. Inc. The house is hers and she is, in fact, turning six and fifty years in the fall. Again, pull the matter from the agenda." Her voice rose to attract even more attention than her cooing at Lisa and Katherine.

Katherine's face lost the taught puckered pull. She shot a look at Lisa, "You said the owner was her son. And we didn't want pity cases swallowing our street."

Lisa opened her mouth then closed it.

"Pity cases?" Adelia whispered.

Lisa stared at her lap. "It wasn't meant to be hurtful. Only that we want neighbors who deserve to be here. Residents who meet the age requirement and financial stability." She glanced up at Adelia, "Our records indicate Franklin, Inc. was registered to your son."

"And you left the digging there." Tanny stated. "You also failed to read the signature on the company's Bylaws agreement." Tanny produced a copy that Christopher had emailed her and slid it across the table to the red-faced women. She pointed to the bottom line, "Please tell me what that says."

"Adelia Franklin," Katherine read. She put her hand over her mouth and sighed. "I am so sorry, Adelia. I truly believed you were taking advantage of our beloved community."

The waiter brought the two soy lattes to the women and placed a flaming trident napkin beneath each beverage. "May I get you ladies anything more?"

"No, thank you," Tanny said, speaking for everyone.

The waiter left and Lisa picked up the latte, holding the Black mug with the word Evil written in red. "I'll pull it from the agenda. The matter is dropped."

Adelia smiled, the tension in her shoulders eased, "Appreciated."

"I do hope you ladies have learned research is a valuable tool. One that has no limitations. Now, on to more pleasant matters." She bit her toast. "At the end of the month Adelia will be making her debut as Savannah Valley's own Art Curator for the art center. She will be opening the new gallery's exhibition with a gala to make her introduction. She is personally inviting you both."

Katherine blew across her stiff foamed beverage. "I'll be there. What artist will you be exhibiting?"

Adelia was caught off guard by the transition of topics. "Rather than a single artist or style, I am focusing on private collections. Those gems kept in vaults by those who would like to share their appreciation with like-minded residents."

"I have a collection," Lisa whispered. "If you would consider one of my pieces, I'll contribute. For what duration are you asking?"

Adelia was stunned. "I figure three-month rotations for now. I have not put out a formal request yet since the gallery is still under renovation. The security installation and free-standing walls are to be delivered soon. What did you have in mind for the display?"

Lisa sipped, "I have a Rogier van der Weyden."

"What?" Adelia blurted. She clasped her hands over her mouth, exasperated by her raw outburst.

Lisa squinted at her. "Yes, I have a Rogier, and your reaction tells me you know what that means."

"Care to share?" Tanny asked.

Katherine seconded Tanny. "Never heard of him. But my collection is mainly contemporary."

Adelia shook her head in disbelief. "Rogier, secular or religious?"

Lisa looked her in the eyes, raised her brow and spoke one word. "Secular."

Adelia sat back hard, her face slack. She fiddled with the napkin in her lap. Shaking her head, she laughed. "Are you telling me you have a lost Rogier?"

The woman nodded.

Adelia spoke to the whole table. "Oh, we're on the same page. The Rogier de la Pasture was a fifteenth century northern renaissance artist born in Tournai. His work, *Descent from the Cross, The Last Judgment*, and *Madonna with the Saints* was a precedent. He was appointed the position of city painter in Brussels after becoming a master painter under Campin. His secular works are said to be lost."

Lisa dropped her façade and stared at the woman in

awe. A smile spread over her face. "I assure you, Mrs. Franklin, Adelia, I do not own that which is common. Everything in my vaults is of the rarest echelon."

Adelia was impressed. She sipped her own latte to keep from smiling at the bitty, now turned intriguing conquest, before her. The possibility of seeing a Rogier forced her to cross her legs to keep from jumping at the woman. Her whole being wanted to grovel for a chance. "I don't suppose you would be open to sharing a glimpse at such a rare treasure?"

Tanny finished her Nutella toast and brushed the crumbs off her fingers with the edge of her napkin. "Ladies, I believe we have the making for one magnificent show. Adelia, you can choose one of my pieces for the objects room. You can choose whatever you see in the penthouse. I don't have a collector's vault."

"Seriously," Katherine interrupted. "You have no precious items?"

Tanny shook her head, "The items I hold dear are not an asset to anyone but myself. I have a collection of my children's items over the course of their childhood and items passed down through the generations in my family and my husband's. When it comes to collecting, I guess my guilt lies in books. I have a Gutenberg Bible, and several first editions."

"Several?" Katherine questioned with a look of disbelief shown through her furrowed brows.

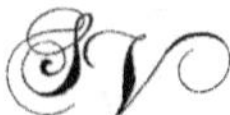

Tanny bit her bottom lip. “Okay, maybe a few scrolls, and a two-story library in the back of the penthouse. But it’s not as elaborate as art.”

Adelia frowned at her. “You do know that literature is a form or art. The books, especially antiquated books, have handwritten pages and many were written by monks and decorated with illuminated pages. They used gold leafing and precious metals to embellish.”

The Rat Pack exchanged a glance and then leaned toward Tanny. Lisa moved her drink aside. “I think you know you have a treasure trove and are teasing us.”

Katherine wriggled in her seat. “Dr. Tanny Willias, you’re pulling our leg.”

Tanny chuckled. “Maybe, just a little.”

The women continued to talk about their collections until the Rat Pack finished their beverages, and Margaret texted Adelia letting her know that she had Josie and was on her way.

Lisa stood, extending her hand to Adelia. “We good?”

Adelia nodded with a smile. “Yeah, we’re good.” She took Lisa’s hand.

Lisa held onto the woman’s pale fingers. The look of shame had vanished from her face though it hung in her voice, “I’m free Thursday morning if you’d like to stop in and view my collection. I may consider contributing on a regular basis. I assume we’ll get some sort of recognition for the work?”

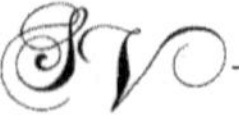

Adelia held back a smirk. "Of course, gold and etched."

The two shameless women Adelia no longer fretted about, disappeared into the Savannah sunshine. The doors closed behind them, opening a new chapter in Adelia's life. One that she felt was charging forward.

"Eh-hem," Tanny coughed.

"Yes?" Adelia obliged. "You tricked me."

"Yes, but with honest intent. It sounds like Adelia Franklin has been found," Tanny chided. "Professional fraud detector and now educator to the uber rich. What will she do next?"

Adelia sipped the last of her gingerbread latte. When Ted died, she thought her life was lost. Of all her children, Christopher observed and fought to give her a new lease on life. He reminded her daughters that she was someone. And lucky for her, all her children wanted to see that woman back.

As Chris said during an evening at Abby's bed and breakfast one evening, "Don't overthink the unknown. It's what drags you down. Dad passing lost you the house, but I still created the company. I'm still an investor. I amassed a fortune before he was diagnosed. No matter his health, I was going to help the parents who showed unconditional love in the only way I knew. Enjoy your retirement—for the both of you. It was what he wanted; you know that."

Adelia glanced up at Tanny with tears wetting her

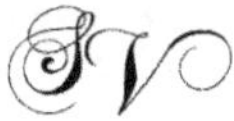

lashes. “My son and I had a code for when it was time to retreat.”

“Oh, do explain,” Tanny encouraged.

“When Chris was young, he was shy. Too shy, people said. But he was like me, and I recognized myself in him. So, we created a secret code for when times were overwhelming. Times when he needed a break or to regroup. I understood because I was . . . no, am the same. When he looked unhappy or tense, I would ask him, Chris what’s the status? And he would say ‘yes’ or ‘no’.” Adelia blotted a tear from her cheek. “Yes, meant he needed a break.”

“And ‘no’ meant everything would be okay,” Tanny finished.

Adelia nodded.

“Well, Adelia my friend, after facing down the rats, and procuring the rarest art in the world, I ask: What’s your status?”

Adelia smiled, looking Tanny in the eye. “The status, Dr. Willias, is ‘no.’”

• • •

After facing down the Rat Pack with the support of Tanny, Adelia stole back to her new home with a light filling her chest and mind. She was relieved and awed. The people she thought would cause her world to crumble managed to build her up higher than she ever expected. Savannah Valley promised to be a place like no other and it delivered.

She knew the kind of peace and serenity that lived in her heart could not be bought, but it came from the intellectual relationships forming below the surface.

Over the course of the next six weeks, while the gallery was under construction and security was reinforced, Margaret joined her in the second story studio for art lessons. They painted in Adelia's garden, and the professor turned curator relished in the fact that she brought out the artist within her friend. She taught Margaret through her art. "Passion is not lost, only put aside. Fashion is art, Margaret," she had said, "Now put those visions on canvas and lose yourself. You don't need me. It's inside of you."

Margaret wept after her first completed work. "I needed you to find me, Adelia. You call it inner passion; I call it a listening friend who draws the best out of you."

Margaret, Josie, and Tanny invaded Adelia's workspace four times in that six-week period. Each bringing with them a preferred wine or box of goodies. It started after Josie suggested a paint and sip when she and Penelope dropped in on Adelia and Margaret painting in the front lawn. She pulled up her Aston Martin two-seater and dropped the sunglasses to the tip of her nose. She sped off, returned with Tanny and a bottle of Bordeaux and the rest was becoming history.

The gallery was set to open and the invitations to the gala were sent. Josie took care of the formalities while

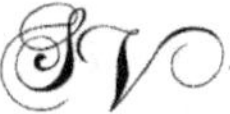

Adelia focused on the show. With the aid of Savannah Valley's concierge service, she found a goldsmith on call who was more than knowledgeable about plaques and famous pieces.

Christopher finally texted her back about contacting Edith, but she was pleased to tell him that she resolved the problem without snitching. He promised to come to her show. In truth Adelia wanted him to meet her new friends.

• • •

"Adelia," Margaret said, stroking Luciano's head the final morning before the show. They were sitting in on the front porch enjoying the morning over coffee.

"Yes," Adelia said.

"I want to give you something," Margaret reassured. "It's nothing formal, wait here. I'll fetch it for you."

Adelia tucked her periwinkle blue dress beneath her thighs and watched Margaret dash away into her lemon pudding house leaving the double arched doors open behind her.

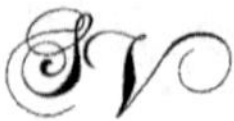

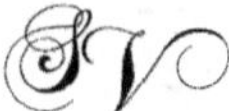

CHAPTER 10

GALA AT THE GALLERY

Margaret returned with her attendant, Gary in tow. He held a hefty white box with a large purple bow. “Surprendre!” Margaret cooed in French. She waved her hands at Gary to put it on table.

Adelia folded her lips to keep from cringing at what her eccentric friend could have given her. She stood and pulled the end of the ribbon to release the bow. “Margaret, you didn’t have to do this.”

“Oh, stop. I told you weeks ago, I love surprises. Come on,” The woman clapped, urging Adelia to work faster.

Adelia let the ribbon fall to the sides and maneuvered the stiff cardboard lid off the even firmer container. It came off in a rush, forcing Adelia to step back. Squeaks filled the air and a bag inside was shaking. “Margaret,” she gasped as she peered inside the mesh screen of the bag. A teensy teacup Yorkie in the tan and black Gucci carry bag yipped up at her. Adelia’s hands shook as she reached to unzip it and lift the hand-sized bundle. “He’s adorable! Is that a diamond studded collar?”

Margaret laughed showing her delight. “The offspring of Luciano and Penelope deserves no less.” She grinned.

“Oh, my goodness,” Adelia squealed at the creature

licking her chin with fervor. She lifted the little thing and peeked to confirm the gender. "It's a girl. I'll have to find the right name for you." Her smile reached glistening eyes as she cuddled the silken puppy.

"Living alone is never easy. A tiny face to warm your heart first thing in the morning keeps you going." Margaret instructed. "Adelia, you are young, and this little babe has a lifetime ahead of her. Penelope has been away at the Savannah Valley birthing retreat for four legged residents."

"Wait, a birthing retreat for pets? I love it. What do they do?" Adelia asked, her eyes focused on the tan body squirming body and pink belly.

"When our dear ones give birth, they get round the clock care by a personal attendant, twenty-four hours a day. Once the young ones are weened, the pups are assigned their own attendant at the doggie day care. And the service comes to the house to house-train and what not." Margaret bragged. "Your little joy is eight weeks old. Penelope went into labor the week you arrived. Josie's been absolutely giddy over her new grand-puppies."

"And you never told me!" Adelia chastised.

"That would have ruined the surprise."

Adelia turned the pup this way and that. There wasn't a speck of black on her. A bit of white hair showed on her chest and her eyes were little ebony stones. "You know, you remind me of bird. Your whimpers are like a morning song, little one." She nuzzled the shining black nose. I'm going to give you a lucky name, one that my Ted nicknamed me the first time he heard me sing. You'll be my Nightingale."

Margaret sat in her chair and blotted her own tears. "Adelia, that's beautiful." She crossed her legs and rested her hands in her lap. The attendant removed the bag from the box and left with the packaging.

"Some say nightingales bring good luck and tranquility," Adelia peered at Margaret. "She has already quieted my heart. Thank you."

Luciano pranced onto the porch. Margaret scooped him into her arms, "Luciano, meet your daughter, Nightingale." She held him in her arm and directed his face toward the little fur ball. Adelia figured he could care less, but Margaret continued, "You'll have to tell Josie tonight. She's been so anxious. The woman has already organized visitation events. If you don't watch out, she'll be planning your baby's first birthday."

• • •

After the eventful morning, Adelia readied for the gala. The week before, the ladies took her to the Savannah Valley shops to find the perfect evening gown. She wound up choosing a gold gown with flowing tulle sleeves that extended to the floor. Her hair stylist arrived at the house with his make up artist in tow. The men airbrushed color on her face, cheeks, and hair. She had false lash bits, and an

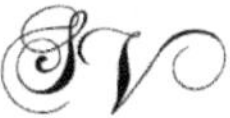

updo. When she peered in the mirror, she didn't recognize herself.

Adelia realized her own metamorphosis that transformed her into the confident woman standing before her. She believed it was because of Christopher and his forethought.

He arrived that afternoon ready to escort his mother to the grand opening. He stepped up behind her wearing a full tailed black tuxedo with a gold paisley best, a perfect match.

"Mom, you look happy." He kissed her cheek.

She hugged him, careful not to get make up on his clothes. "Never in my wildest dreams did I imagine retirement would see me back to work and enjoying life while doing it. When people talk about retiring, it's always about getting away and not having any more responsibilities. But, Chris, that's not it at all. At least for me. It feels good to be wanted, not just needed."

He kissed her head and picked up the Gucci bag with the sleeping pup. "Is she joining us this evening?"

"Of course, it's what the rich do, I hear." She smiled; her red lips parted.

"Ah, so you're rich now? You wear it well."

They laughed and carried the pup to the waiting black limo. The gallery would open in fifty-nine minutes. Adelia already spent the better part of the day in the building ensuring all the pieces were marked, the security system worked, and the caterers set up the tables under the massive tent in front of the art center where a spilled glass wouldn't risk doom to any one of the rare pieces.

The chauffeur pulled the car to the entrance and opened the door. Adelia stepped out assisted by her attendant. Margaret insisted she have her own transportation in case of an emergency and to assist with puppy care. Savannah Valley provided the assistants, but Adelia never thought it necessary until Margaret jokingly mentioned Adelia's fear of getting trapped in the glass elevator.

Margaret liked to remind her of the incident. "If I hadn't come for you, who knows how long you'd have been in there. You should have seen the horror on your precious face."

Adelia smiled recalling her standard response. "That thing will be the death of me." After that, Adelia called the service line to save her from the glass enclosure.

"What are you thinking about, mom?" Christopher asked as he emerged from the car. He put his arm out for his mother as he carried the bag with his new fur-laden sibling.

Adelia blew a kiss to the little face watching through the mesh window. "Nothing in particular. Just how grateful I am for you and for the world you opened for me."

The glass cubed building dazzled with colored lights.

In front was a metal sculpture that reminded Adelia of a sea creature floating through water. It was perfect. The magnitude of her venture struck home. She was the curator of a gallery filled with priceless art pieces: a Ming vase from Tanny, a Renoir by Goddard, Patricia from the theatrical group offered a Picasso, while Ruby, the angel of Savannah Valley, provided a Jackson Pollock. She had Lisa's Rogier which stunned her beyond words as the focal piece situated at the end of the gallery. There was even a Van Gogh from Edith and others from residents eager to reveal their prize possessions.

"Mom, do any of these people appreciate what they have and what they are leaving for their children and grandchildren?" Christopher asked.

"I suspect some do but not all. They don't have a son as wise as you to teach them about generational wealth. Come on, we have a party to attend."

As per Adelia's request, each resident attending the gala purchased a ticket worth fifty thousand dollars to go to a charity of their choosing.

"Before we go in, let's check out the dining area." She led him into the tent where the tables were set with sterling silverware, Waterford crystal glasses and Wedgwood China. The centerpieces consisted of overflowing vases of white roses and green stemmed cattails place settings.

Programs bound in faux leather were placed at each

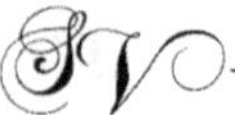

setting. Each of the fifty tables provided seating for six. Black linens and white candles provided the elegance Adelia sought. It reminded her of the chorale's performance rekindling the goosebumps on her arms.

Plumes of pussy willows and white lights anchored the corners of the garden.

The tables formed a circle around an eight-foot ice sculpture replicating the Savannah Valley logo. And next to the ice sculpture was a small platform stage, shiny and new. The floor had yet to be marred by high heels from other events. She would be the first to grace its stage.

"Mom, it's magnificent."

The catering manager brought a tasting plate for Adelia and Chris to view and sample. She bit the salmon mousse filled phyllo, and the caviar topped toasts. There were tomato and mozzarella bits on picks, peach and chicken filled lettuce leaves, and two bite brownies.

"It's all delicious," she told the man waiting to hear her criticisms. "It's more than I expected, thank you."

The gentleman bowed. "I must thank you, madame. For it is high praise. Enjoy your show." He retreated behind a curtained area waving for several members of the wait-staff to follow.

She squeezed Christopher's arm, "It's perfect. Let's go inside."

She watched as Christopher took it all in as they entered

the building. The dome-like lobby ceiling was painted sky blue and recessed lights twinkled down reflecting off the polished marble floor. An architectural replica of the art center sat on a custom teak platform in the middle of the lobby. In front of the display the bright yellow ribbon was draped, spanning the width, and a pair of oversized scissors lay on the corner of the platform, ready for Adelia to dedicate the new facility.

They moved into the gallery while a photographer for the *Savannah Valley Times* snapped a photo of Adelia observing the Rogier. Adelia proudly showed Chris where she had painted a flat black tree on a plain white wall. It was a silhouette of a magnolia tree in full bloom. "I worked with the goldsmith to create plaques for each donor to resemble flower petals. It's my gift to those who supported this quest."

"Nice touch, mom?" Christopher's phone rang. He withdrew the device from his jacket pocket hustling from the room. Adelia watched him, curious and a tad worried.

Josie, Margaret, and Tanny entered from the private side entrance. They wore pink satin jackets over their sequined gowns in various shades of pink. Josie had a bag on her arm. She set it by Adelia and withdrew a fourth jacket.

Adelia laughed, "Oh, my God. The Pink Panthers!" She hugged it to her chest. "I love it. Tanny took it from her and draped it over her shoulders while Margaret urged the photographer to take their pictures. Tanny stood on the right, Josie on the left, and Margaret squatted in pose in front of Adelia with her back to the camera to show off the name but turned her head enough for the camera to catch her broad grin.

The photographer took numerous shots while the women posed. In the final one, Josie held Nightingale. The alarm sounded on her phone, and she reached inside her sleeve to turn it off.

"Are you ready?" Tanny asked.

"Yeah, I think I am," Adelia answered, her voice a nervous rasp. They returned to the lobby and joined the owners, known as the Rich Widows of Savannah Valley. Together they exited the building and joined the guests who had filled the tent.

Adelia sat with her entourage, Gill, and Gill's wife, June.

"Dr. Franklin," Gill said. "I wanted to thank you in person. Your alert eyes saved me $2.5 million. Botan House made the deposit this morning." He turned to his wife. "Adelia, this is my wife June. She too, was excited to own a Nicholson and offered an afterthought to our situation."

Adelia settled in her seat with Nightingale's carry bag on her lap. "What is it, Mrs. Berm?"

"As you can imagine, we were gravely disappointed, not

to mention humiliated. We will not be doing business with Botan House in the future. We wondered if you would procure a Nicholson for our wall. I want a relief and am willing to pay any price to have one." She folded her hands on her lap as she spoke. "I trust your judgment and expertise."

Adelia started to comment, but Gill interrupted her with the raise of a finger. "I want to offer you my Rembrandt for one year. It is the least I can do."

Margaret slid the purse from Adelia's lap and removed the tiny pup. "Adelia, Edith is about to introduce you. Why don't you add Mr. Berm's offer to the top of the waiting list?"

Edith's voice sounded through the murmur filled room. "Good evening, all."

The guests responded in kind, "Good evening."

"Tonight, I want to introduce our newest addition to Savannah Valley. She's a woman with brains, guts, and a heart of platinum." She winked at the audience. "We all know platinum's value exceeds that of gold. Please welcome the one and only, Dr. Adelia Franklin, Ph.D., retired department chair at Dartmouth University, procurer, and curator of fine art." She clapped her hands starting a round of thunderous applause as Adelia tucked her tiny companion in her arm and climbed to the stage.

"Thank you, all," Adelia said. The tent quieted. "This evening, I want to welcome you all to the first exhibition at the Savannah Valley Fine Arts gallery. The inspiration for such a show stemmed from a simple newspaper photo. One that captured my attention from day one, a picture that was not about art, but should have been." She shifted the pup to the front and pet the feathery fur covering the darling's ears. The action quieted the excitement coursing through her veins. "While getting to know my neighbors, I learned about private collections in darkened rooms. Pieces in homes with no visitors. It broke my heart to see the life's work of Rembrandt, Picasso, Monet, Pollack, and Rogier go unshared. For art is a gift for the soul. It speaks to all. Some hate it, some love it, but either way it evokes emotion."

The guests laughed.

"Tonight, we have pieces from those hidden places. We offer their artists a spotlight honoring the hours, days, months, weeks," she paused, "and years they toiled to create the final work we have before us. As the program states, we have a secular Rogier on display. It is the rarest of his works." She waited for the sound of guests discussing the work pictured inside the leather binding. "On the pages of your programs, you will find information about the owner, the artist, and the era. You will also find a link to a waiting list for future exhibitions. And, as inspired by the glorious magnolias, I've created a wall of recognition. Each resident will have a gold plaque with their name and artist's work engraved and placed on the magnolia silhouette in the entrance to the gallery."

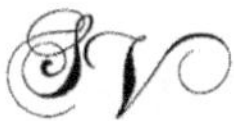

A rush of enthusiasm spread through the tables. Tanny stood, clapping. Margaret, Josie, Gill, and June followed. The waitstaff lined the walls with covered dishes—Adelia's cue to end her speech.

"Again, thank you for coming and supporting your chosen charities." Adelia stood to the side of the four owners awaiting her final initiation as curator.

"And now, Dr. Adelia Franklin, on behalf of Glenda, Darcy, Sharon and myself, as well as the grateful residents of Savannah Valley, it is our pleasure to name you first curator of the Savannah Valley Galleries," Edith handed Adelia a glass of champagne raised her own in a toast. When the applause died down, dinner was served.

As everyone finished their dessert and coffee, Adelia returned to the dais, tapping on the microphone. She searched the room looking for Chris but he hadn't returned.

When the noise settled, she continued. "Now, if you would follow us, we will have our official ribbon cutting in the lobby as we present your new gallery."

Margaret ran to the stage and took Nightingale from Adelia's arms. "You did it, Adelia. Go enjoy the big moment," she whispered as she scurried off, Nightingale in hand.

It took a few moments for the patrons to fill the lobby. Those who couldn't fit stood just outside the open doors. Edith handed Adelia the scissors.

They paused briefly for a photo, then Adelia snipped

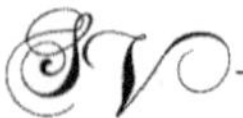

the ribbon. Everyone cheered and filed into the space bearing some of the most treasured art pieces on the planet. Christopher, Margaret, Josie, and Tanny took turns hugging Adelia. She held back tears grateful for the choices she made throughout her life. She remained strong, took risks, sometimes crashed, but it was her perseverance that saw her through. She laughed knowing her younger self would be proud. She worked hard for what she had achieved.

Through the sea of faces she caught a glimpse of Christopher walking through the front door. His face broke into a smile, and he moved to the side. Behind him appeared the three radiant faces of her beloved daughters.

Charlotte, Samantha and Michelle rushed to her side and embraced their mother, tears streaming down their faces.

"What? How? I can't believe . . ." Adelia stammered

"Since when are you at a loss for words?" Christopher chided as he joined them. "You didn't think this night would slip away without your entire tribe here to support you?"

"Is that what that call was about?" Adelia asked.

"Just tending to last minute details. It was hard to drag my sisters away from your new home."

"Our home. I may be the senior in residence, but wherever I am it will always be your home." She embraced each of her in children in turn before announcing, "I think it's high time I taught you a little bit about fine art. Follow me!"

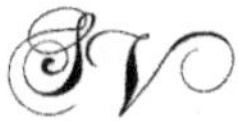

EPILOGUE

Maya Angelou stated it well. “People will forget what you said, people will forget what you did, but people will never forget how you made them feel.”

What the future holds for Adelia is for her to choose. Not only in the actions she takes going forward, and the friends she lets into her life, but also in how she allows them to impact how she feels. The choice is hers. It’s an empowering feeling. No longer will she live under a rock of fear or uncertainly. But instead go on to do great things for herself, her community and her family.

Nightingale is a story of living our best life. We can either choose the ‘fly by the seat of our pants’ approach which provides little-to-no security nor opportunity. Or we can plan for life-events to provide opportunity for a fulfilling and rewarding life.

I’m happy to share that all of Adelia’s children are doing well personally and financially. Having learned from Adelia’s teachings they now carry the torch to have a fulfilling life themselves and equally important to share the teachings with friends, family and the next generation.

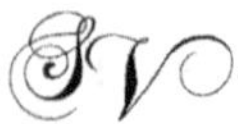

ABOUT TONY LOPES

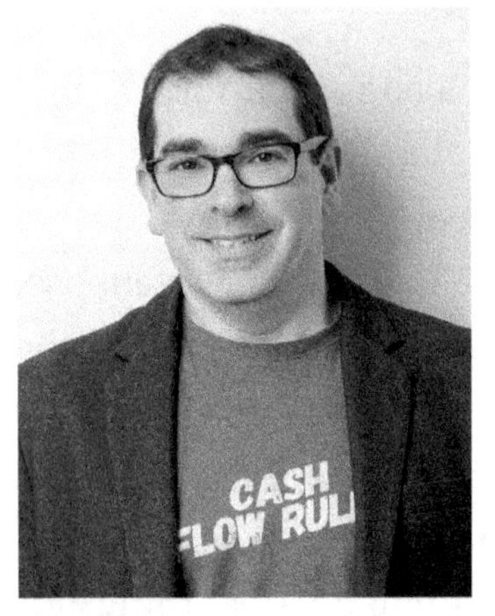

Tony Lopes is a first-generation American, investor, consultant, real estate professional, author, and macroeconomic enthusiast. He earned a BS in Mechanical Engineering and an MBA from UMass.

Tony worked in the defense industry for 19 years in various leadership positions managing multi-million dollar programs while simultaneously building a portfolio of residential income properties. His investments, coupled with his understanding of markets and economics allowed him to retire at age 44.

He now coaches others who are seeking a more enjoyable life with greater freedoms. Tony's journey has given him valuable insight into the topics and teachings provided in this book.

For more info on Tony check out **DirtyBootsCapital.com** or email him at **TonyLopes@DirtyBootsCapital.com**

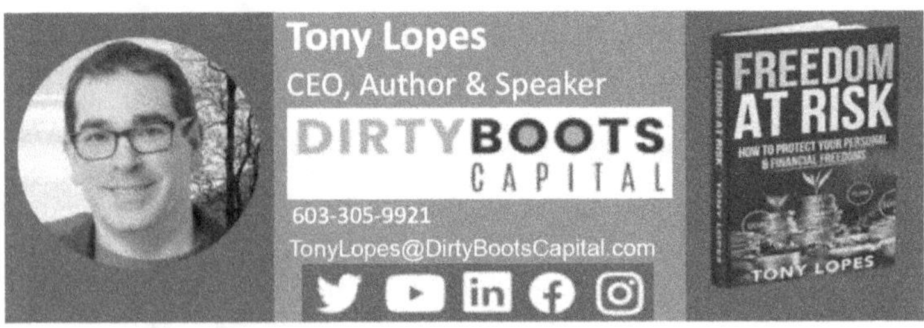

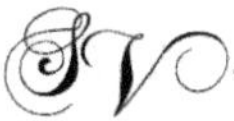

REVIEW

Please leave a review. It would mean so much to me. I want to share the story of someone who was made to feel insecure because she wasn't rich enough. Then she taught those people that she had more wealth in her abilities than they ever dreamed of.

We can all learn to trust ourselves and learn how to protect our own personal and financial freedoms. If you leave a review, someone may be enticed to read my story and learn a whole new way of living.

https://www.amazon.com/Nightingale-Goodby-Yesterday-Tony-Lopes-ebook/dp/B0BC2N3FTV/

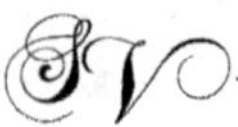

www.ingramcontent.com/pod-product-compliance
Lightning Source LLC
LaVergne TN
LVHW010621100826
845148LV00014B/3069

* 9 7 9 8 8 8 5 8 1 0 5 7 9 *